Easy Interval Method

Klaas Lok

Easy Interval Method

Colophon

Cover photo:
1500m in Nijmegen, the Netherlands, 24-06-1979: Klaas Lok leading with Steve Ovett - five-time world record holder 1500m/Mile & Olympic champion over 800m in 1980 - in hot pursuit; Ovett was first in 3:37.4, with Lok fifth in 3:40.3. (Photo: Theo van de Rakt).

English Language edition first published in the United Kingdom in May 2019 by The Choir Press, Gloucester, United Kingdom.
First published in the Netherlands in 2005 by Klaas Lok
For ordering and questions: www.easyintervalmethod.com

Translated by **Russ Mullen**, West Sussex, United Kingdom
Illustrations, layout and design: **Reinier Mathijsen**, Zeist, the Netherlands

ISBN: 978-1-78963-072-5

*Gratitude to my former coach **Herman Verheul** and to all the runners who contributed with stories about their personal experiences.*
*My special gratitude goes to **Russ Mullen** from Sussex - England, who not only wrote a chapter but also helped me translating this book.*

Klaas Lok

Foreword

For most runners, the thrill and satisfaction of the simple act of running holds our attention for only so long. It is quickly consumed by the desire not only to run but to run faster! Whether you are a novice just trying to run an entire 5km or an elite dreaming of breaking 30 minutes for 10km, the goal is the same: it must be faster.

Running is one of the few sports where success and failure can be so black and white. Most people will never win a race against others. But you will never stop racing against yourself. If you complete the same course 10 seconds quicker than you ever have before, then you have undeniable evidence that you have improved. You've beaten yourself; you win. Conversely, the damning and bleak reality of failure is equally harsh. You didn't win. But you will be back. All runners, no matter what their level, share these common feelings of success and failure and the single-minded determination that you will, one day, be faster than you were before.

I had been running competitively for nearly 10 years and managed to run times ranging from 9:35 (3km), 16:15 (5km), 33:29 (10km) and 1:15:11 (half marathon). I ran these in 2014 at 28 years old and had stagnated since then; actually, if brutally honest, regressed. I would constantly feel sluggish and slow and never ran a race I was happy with for three years. This all changed thanks to a completely different way of training: the Easy Interval Training Method.

I first came across the Easy Interval Method in December 2016 and was immediately intrigued. Within six months of training this way I have since run 3km in 8:59, 5km in 15:44 and 10km in 32:51. I have been *truly* amazed by these improvements as I've not only got back to my previous best but I have surpassed it at every distance I've run. I feel stronger, healthier and happier about all aspects of my running. You can read more about my story in chapter 2.2.

In this book you will read everything about this unique way of training. It is written by a man who has trained and competed at a level that most can only dream of. Klaas Lok won a staggering 24 Dutch titles from 1975 to 1985, and achieved times that, even today, would still rank him in the upper echelons of the world's elite distance runners.

Russ Mullen

In the following pages Klaas shares his first-hand knowledge and experience of competing and training at a world-class level with a goal that all runners, no matter how fast or slow, can share: the goal to be faster than you were before. His insights provide thoughtful and unique ideas into the approach he personally used under the tutelage of his coach, Herman Verheul, and while there are no guarantees that following these ideas will turn you into a national champion, I do believe they will provide a thought-provoking insight into a unique and intuitive way of training that will lead to improved performance, health and enjoyment in your running, whatever your level.

Russ Mullen, Haywards Heath Harriers, Sussex, UK

Klaas Lok (212) finishes 2nd in the European Indoor Championships in 1980. Karl Fleschen (Germany; no 365) wins, Hans-Jürgen Orthmann (Germany) takes bronze. Photo: Theo van de Rakt

1. Introduction

Hello, my name is Klaas Lok. I am a former middle and long-distance runner from the Netherlands. I have won 24 national distance titles across a variety of terrains and a range of distances, including six cross-country titles. I achieved times including 10,000m in 28:24 and 1500m in 3:38.8. I was also fortunate enough to hold two Dutch records, finish second in the European Indoor Championship 3000m (1980) and 20th in the World Cross-Country Championships in 1980.

Results World Cross-Country championships 1980 in Paris.

1	Craig Virgin	United States	37:01	16	Fernando Mamede	Portugal	37:42
2	Hans-Jürgen Orthmann	West Germany	37:02	17	Steve Kenyon	England	37:44
3	Nick Rose	England	37:05	18	John Treacy	Ireland	37:44
4	Léon Schots	Belgium	37:11	19	Nick Lees	England	37:47
5	John Robson	Scotland	37:20	20	Klaas Lok	Netherlands	37:48
6	Aleksandr Antipov	Soviet Union	37:21	21	Alex Hagelsteens	Belgium	37:49
7	Leonid Moseyev	Soviet Union	37:21	22	José Luis González	Spain	37:51
8	Antonio Prieto	Spain	37:21	23	Kenneth Martin	United States	37:53
9	Steve Jones	Wales	37:23	24	Dominique Coux	France	37:54
10	Bernie Ford	England	37:25	25	Alex Gonzalez	France	37:54
11	Karel Lismont	Belgium	37:27	26	Carlos Lopes	Portugal	37:55
12	Daniel Dillon	United States	37:28	27	François Person	France	37:55
13	El Hachami Abdenouz	Algeria	37:31	28	Valeriy Sapon	Soviet Union	37:56
14	Barry Smith	England	37:33	29	Allister Hutton	Scotland	37:57
15	Thierry Watrice	France	37:39	30	José Sena	Portugal	37:59

During my career, I ran with some of the finest athletes who have ever graced our sport, including the great Steve Ovett. Unfortunately, I was no match for a man whose ability far exceeded my own (Steve could run a 200m in 21.7 seconds, while my best was around 25), but I still consider it an honour to have lined up and competed against such a formidable opponent.

I wasn't talented; the Easy Interval Method made me a champion

When I first started training seriously I used a more 'traditional' approach, which included fast endurance runs (actually tempo runs) and very hard interval sessions of 200-400m, often at my maximum capacity. If I wanted to improve, I needed to push myself harder, surely? As a result, at the age of 18, I achieved times of 4:17 for 1500m and 9:20 for 3000m. While these times are perfectly respectable, they don't show any hint of world-class talent. Consider that former 5000m world record holder and 1984 Olympic champion Said Aouita ran his first 3000m in 8:15 (as an 18-year-old football player during a fitness test) and you'll see a huge contrast in ability at a young age. As an 18-year-old I ran just 13.5 seconds over 100m (most elite 1500m runners are capable of 11.5 or faster). Five years later I improved to 12.5 at 100m, but it still illustrates that I wasn't a great natural talent from a young age - as some people want to make out.

The purpose of this book is to tell you about a very special and unique training method which took me from a regional also-ran to a national champion. This method is renowned (and controversial) in the Netherlands and is slowly finding new proponents elsewhere around the globe. Many people react with surprise and disbelief when they first hear about it, but most of the runners who start training according to this method, stick to it for the rest of their career. I am talking about the so-called 'Easy Interval Method', whose spiritual father is Herman Verheul (1932-2012), my coach in the Netherlands during my own career. It flies in the face of many of the set-in-stone training ideas and methodologies that are commonly accepted amongst distance runners, but I urge you to read on with an open mind and hope that you can implement some of the ideas presented to help improve your own running.

Herman Verheul developed a way of training which, during my career (more modern coaches are implementing slower, relaxed interval training), stood directly opposite the teachings of most of the established 'running schools'. Starting in the 1960s the 'long distance training' approach was generally adopted. Nearly all athletic clubs accepted the common belief that the majority of training should be steady-state runs of various distances (including the traditional 'two hour long run' on Sunday). This was complemented with the hard, anaerobic interval/tempo workouts twice a week.

Verheul's ideas went against nearly everything commonly accepted as the 'correct' way of training. He noticed that many athletes had developed a 'heavy' running style as a result of their high-volume training and longer, slower runs. When an athlete is training so much it is impossible to run at a quick speed or high intensity due to risk of injury and so they are forced to slow down their daily paces. Alongside this, he didn't believe that two hard speed (anaerobic) interval/tempo workouts added to a weekly race could benefit the performance of most of the runners. The slower paces of their regular training meant that their interval sessions were often incredibly intense, which put the runner at a greater risk of injury and especially fatigue.

Instead of slow endurance training as the basis of all training, Verheul introduced a basic training consisting of relaxed, easy interval training. He was inspired by the interval training of two famous coaches of the post-war era. Hungarian coach Mihály Iglói and German Woldemar Gerschler, both of whom coached world record holders in the 1950s, were Verheul's main source of inspiration, while he also had an eye for the training of the great Emil Zatopek (four times Olympic champion from 1948-1952). The training of Iglói though - whose athletes were full-time runners - was much heavier than Verheul thought was appropriate for his runners: students and workers with full-time jobs.

Over the course of nearly a decade, Verheul discovered that a more relaxed basic training gave even better results. For example, in the late 1960s his best 1500m runner (3:47) did his basic 400m-workouts in 68 seconds, but by the mid-1970s I (Klaas Lok - 3:38) ran them in just 75 (in winter) and generally around 72-70 seconds (in summer).

The core of the Easy Interval Method consists of many relaxed, extensive interval sessions over distances of 200m, 400m, and 1000m (other distances like 500m, mile and 2000m can also be used), which have to be run in a much more relaxed and slower way than most traditional interval sessions. These sessions could almost be considered as more or less aerobic runs with surges or easy structured fartleks, especially the 400 and 1000m intervals. It can be compared with the aerobic interval training made famous by Emil Zatopek, and should not be compared with hard anaerobic interval sessions.

Once a week, during pre-race build-up periods, there is a harder mixed session (1.5 to 2 hours) in the forest in which one finds a mix of distances from 50m at max speed, all the way up to 2-3km, hill training, aerobic tempos, anaerobic tempos, sprints and whole-body core and conditioning exercises. This session is probably the only one during that week that is deemed as 'hard' or anaerobic in nature. Most other coaches allowed their runners to train anaerobically several times a week.

Sustained steady-state runs are non-existent in the Easy Interval Method. Only during weekends without a race or for runners who train for long distances such as a marathon will a longer, sustained run (but with surges!) be required. Verheul almost completely opposed any long runs for 800-1500m runners (he preferred cross-country races) and in race periods these runs were totally discarded. Last but not least, the Easy Interval Method demands a high frequency of racing. The possibility of running a race almost every weekend over various distances is precisely what makes this method perfect for the runner who gets the most fun and enjoyment out of racing.

Differences
Some main differences compared to traditional methods (which are based on high mileage, steady-state training):
• Most of the steady-state runs are replaced by easy interval training or (sometimes) a long run with surges.
• For athletes racing: not two but just one weekly anaerobic workout and in a period of many races even none (the race is often the 'anaerobic session').
• Some speed during every session (running fast every day).

Some advantages of the Easy Interval Method as experienced by users:
• Lighter training programme.
• More fun in training.
• More reactivity in their legs (which gives a better running economy and improved biomechanics when running); better finishing sprint; feeling more powerful and lighter on their feet.
• Being able to run at higher speed without acidification (lactate) in the muscles.
• Most runners report fewer injuries (once used to this way of training).
• Better training for older and masters runners to maintain speed and reactive running.

- Fitter and better prepared before races.
- Faster recovery after races.
- Able to run more races.
- Looking forward to each training session.
- A middle-distance runner only needs to do around 30% or less of the heavy anaerobic training compared to 'traditional' training runners.
- Much quicker return to fitness after a period of not training, after illness or injury.

Easy Interval Method: suitable for all runners, including beginners

This book is not just aimed at elite runners or competitive athletes. It is important to emphasise that this idea of training works well for all levels and for all runners who are looking to improve their times. For example, runners who are looking to run 10km in under an hour can read the story of a fellow athlete who struggled for years to break 52 minutes. I have real world examples of runners who achieved this and you can read their inspiring stories in chapter 2.2.

This method is also very suitable for novice runners. A traditional training plan for a beginner is mostly aimed at achieving the ability to run non-stop for a certain distance. After a year or so they might be able to run for an hour without any problems and they are happy and proud with their progress. But, unfortunately, they don't realise that they are not training in the most efficient way. There is a chance that they have joined the large number of runners who have reduced their reactivity, running style, coordination and natural speed: they have learned perfectly how to run slowly instead of practicing how to run fast! With the Easy Interval Method beginners will not only be increasing their stamina to be able to run longer, they will also be learning to run faster and more efficiently at the same time.

Easy Interval Method: also applicable for older runners

Some - or maybe many - coaches believe that older runners shouldn't do much interval training and should mainly focus on steady-state training, because the muscle reactivity of masters runners is declining. My opinion is completely different: reactivity - which is so basic and essential for running - should be maintained at your personal highest level. Not only are strong, reactive muscles faster, they are also less prone to injury. Many masters runners who changed to this way of training reported that - after carefully building up and getting used to more mileage at higher speed - they have fewer injuries and perform better. It is widely accepted that it is not the aerobic system that declines so much with age as it is the ability and reactivity of the muscles. To keep that ability for as long as possible, we must train them in the appropriate way. Longer, slower, steady-state running only further reduces their natural reactivity and explosiveness.

It isn't a coincidence that masters runner John van der Wansem from the Netherlands ran world and European records in the age group 40+ and 50+. And let's not forget German runner Silke Schmidt (living in the Netherlands and training according to the Easy Interval Method) who ran seven world records in the age group 55+ .

The Easy Interval Method can serve as a basis for all distances from 800m up to half marathon, and can even be used in a marathon preparation. Of course, not all of us can be national champions and one runner may respond better than another, but history has so far told me that the majority of people who have attempted this idea of training are running faster and stronger than ever before and, perhaps most importantly, report a sense of enjoyment they'd long since lost from running.

Many report they feel freed from the burden of huge weekly volumes and endless slower runs. That is not to say that steady-state runs are not enjoyable or beneficial for some runners. They can increase your aerobic fitness, but you won't benefit fully - and perhaps not at all - when you don't compensate all the slow mileage by a lot of fast interval training and explosive exercises such as hopping and bounding. Unfortunately, so many runners don't have enough time and energy to do all these things alongside their steady-state training. This could result in, for example, a 42-minute 10km runner, doing five workouts a week, training 60km steady-state with just 6-8km intervals, having the aerobic fitness to run 40 minutes, but the lack of power and reactivity in their legs mean they fall short of their potential. The Easy Interval Method can solve this problem.

As with all changes in training, begin gradually and change step by step. If you are mainly used to running long and steady it will be a big change to touch faster speeds every day and it will take your muscles time to adapt. Start with running the intervals even slower than is prescribed in this book and build up the number of repetitions gradually. Be patient, the results are worth it. Please read on and discover how you (most of you) can run faster with less effort. I hope you will enjoy the book and your 'easy interval running', and hopefully you will reach a new level of performance that you never thought possible!

Coach Herman Verheul,
clubmate Ad Buijs
(10,000m in 29:09),
Klaas Lok and clubmate
Joost Borm (1500m
3:38) in 1979
Photo: archive of Klaas Lok

2.1 Successes

During my career I performed consistently well at a high level. However, many other Dutch runners have achieved national and international standards at both senior and masters level using the Easy Interval Method.

I ran for the AV Phoenix club in Utrecht during my prime years and I was not the only one in my club having success. John van der Wansem was one of the leading masters in the world from 1990-2005 and has achieved two 40+ and one 55+ world records. His story is outlined in chapter 2.2. Ad Buijs (10,000m in 29:11) and Joost Borm (1500m in 3:38, multiple Dutch champion and 2000m record holder for over 20 years) both represented the Netherlands at the elite level. Other former clubmates have gone on to very successful coaching careers, all basing their training philosophy on the initial ideas of Verheul. Two of those - Lex van Eck van der Sluijs and Piet de Peuter - were very successful with national, world and Olympic champions.

Lex van Eck van der Sluijs began coaching in the city of The Hague (Netherlands) and produced a number of top-class runners who gathered dozens of national titles, two Dutch records and masters world titles and records. His best-known athlete is the incredible German runner Silke Schmidt. In 2015 she was named 'IAAF Female Master Athlete of the Year'. During an amazing 12 months she won four world titles and ran seven world records in the 55+ age category. Other notable athletes under Lex's guidance were Patrick Aris (3000m in 7:57, 5000m in 13:47), Huub Pragt (Dutch marathon champion), Joke Kleijweg (Dutch 10,000m champion, winner of the 1991 Rotterdam Marathon in 2:34:18, Carlien Harms (Dutch cross-country champion, record holder over 10,000m in 32:22.8) and Erica van de Bilt (5000m national champion in 15:23.27). Finally, Wilma van Onna won several big road races in America while being coached by Lex. These runners may not be right at the top of the world's elite but they all improved significantly after adopting the Easy Interval Method, and achieved times and success that they never thought possible.

Joke Kleijweg in 3rd position during a 10km road race. She won the Rotterdam Marathon in 1991 in 2:34:18
Photo: archive Joke Kleijweg

Olympic champion and two world champions

In 2009, Piet de Peuter moved to the small Kenyan village of Keringet, which sits more than 2600m above sea level. He initially went to Kenya to escape the busy Western lifestyle and help the local population, but he soon found himself coaching a group of talented young athletes, including the then unknown 15-year-old Faith Kipyegon. With almost no resources he produced several world-class runners and even Olympic and world champions: Faith Kipyegon (Kenyan cross-country champion, 2016 Olympic 1500m gold medallist, 1500m world champion in 2017), Geoffrey Kirui (10,000m in 26:55, marathon world champion in 2017). Interestingly, despite being a marathon runner, Geoffrey only ran 100–120km a week and did just four long runs of 40km in his preparation before the world championships. Mercy Chebwogen and Gilbert Kirui (brother of Geoffrey) both won medals at the world junior championships over 3000m and 3000m steeplechase respectively.

Geoffrey Kirui, leading during a workout in Keringet, while preparing for the Chicago Marathon 2018
Photos left: archive Piet de Peuter

Faith Kipyegon, 2016 Olympic and 2017 world champion 1500m, with coach Piet de Peuter. Photo: Veron Lust

Another notable improvement came from Berthold Berger. As a young runner, Berthold was told by his coach that he would never run under four minutes for 1500m and advised him to concentrate on longer distances. Berthold was not to be put off and, after making contact with me, he changed his training dramatically, moving away from the traditional steady running approach to the Easy Interval Method. Two years later, under my guidance, Berthold ran 1500m in 3:43 and won a silver medal at the Dutch Indoor Championships over 3000m. Needless to say, Berthold never went back to his old training.

Bram Som won the European Championships over 800m in 2006. At the time he was training in a more traditional way, with steady endurance runs and hard tempo training. His personal best time was 1:43:45 (Dutch record). While he achieved great success, he eventually fell foul to many injuries and had multiple surgeries. When he finally returned to training he adopted the Easy Interval Method under his brother-in-law and new coach, Ruben Jongkind (another former Phoenix Utrecht athlete). With much less volume and intensity in training, Bram lowered his personal bests of 400m to 46.55, 1000m to 2:17.01 and 1500m to 3:42.75. He also ran 800m in 1:43.59, almost breaking his own record. Given the injuries and the fact that Bram was already at world class level (and three years older!) these are remarkable achievements. Bram says of his training: "Now I realise that actually in those days I wasn't training as an 800m runner but more as a 10km runner, and my running style showed this. After one year training with the Easy Interval Method as basic training I could run at a higher pace in a much more relaxed way and I felt more power in my legs". In chapter 11, about 800m training, you will find a comparison between his old and new schedule.

2.2   Personal stories

The following chapter includes some real-life stories and experiences of runners of all different levels, from national-class athletes to beginners. Even though their speeds may vary greatly there are many common elements that tie their stories together. Specifically the surprise of running faster with less training!

Jaap Vallentgoed (x8) wins Dutch masters cross-country title in 1993

Photo: archive Jaap Vallentgoed

Jaap Valentgoed (1946)

Dutch masters champion 45+ marathon and cross-country 1993

"During the first half of my career my training mainly consisted of long endurance runs with two fast interval sessions. I was focussed on mileage, mostly around 120 to 140km a week. I achieved reasonably satisfying results. Soon after changing to the Easy Interval Method with Klaas, I noticed a change in running style and strength. My push-off got stronger and more reactive. This was especially noticeable on the track and in cross-country races. My finishing speed also improved a lot! I enjoyed the different approach of training for the marathon – a faster 200 or 400m every six minutes instead of the monotonous slow run of two hours. I noticed that after these runs I didn't have the languid feeling that I was used to after my usual slow 2-2.5 hour runs. The next day my legs also felt a lot better. I lowered my best marathon time by four minutes and won the Dutch masters title. In my opinion, this method is very suitable for masters runners, because with a lot of easy interval training one keeps their reactivity at a good level, as I noticed myself."

Photo: archive
Erika van de Bilt

Erika van de Bilt (1971)

Dutch 5000m champion in 2000; 5000m in 15:23

As a youngster, Erika was a talented runner. At just 17 years old she came from triathlon training to run a sub 38-minute 10km road race. Her coach at the time saw her talent in running and advised her to build up her mileage with a lot of steady-state running. Unfortunately, the result was that her running style deteriorated and she drifted into obscurity. She then changed her coach to Frans Thuys (coach of 1992 Olympic 800m champion Ellen van Langen and Christine Toonstra - former Dutch 10,000m record holder in 31:45). This resulted in a return to some sort of form, but Erika's real breakthrough came after she switched to coach Lex van Eck van der Sluijs - an easy interval advocate. She went from being in the middle of the pack to a national champion over 5000m and lowered her 5000m time from 16:40 to 15:23, her 1500m down to 4:15 and half marathon to 1:14:21. She also competed in the world cross-country championships and in the Golden League in Berlin. Erika's talent was there from an early age but, unfortunately, it wasn't until she trained using the Easy Interval Method that her potential was finally realised.

She said in 2001: "At first I thought it was a bit odd, training relatively relaxed tempos every day and just once a week some harder tempos during a mixed session in the forest. However, at a certain moment I felt how much my 'running movement' improved and during a long period I ran a personal best in almost every race. I was then convinced by this method of training. It was also remarkable how much my finishing sprint improved!"

John van der Wansem (1950)

Former world record holder masters 40+ in 1990: 3000m (8:15.5) and 1 hour run (18,919m); world record holder masters 55+: 1 hour run 17,394m (2005)

John has been one of the top masters runners in the Netherlands for two decades (1990-2010). At the start of his career he won several medals at Dutch championships and made the national team. Unfortunately, due to injuries he stopped running at the top level at only 25 years old. It wasn't until he was 32 that he began training again. As a masters runner he was even more successful, breaking several world records.

What is most remarkable is that, as a young runner, John trained according to the Lydiard-method with very high mileage. At age 35 he switched to the Easy Interval Method and ran a personal best for 10,000m as a 38-year-old! When taking age-related performances into account, virtually all of John's achievements during later years are far superior to those in his younger days. For example, 14:21.6 for 5000m as a 40+ runner is similar to a 13:49 for a 25-year-old - better than the 13:55.6 that he actually ran when he was 24. His 10km time of 31:49 which he ran as a sprightly 51-year-old is equivalent to a 28:20 of a 25-year-old.

Compare his schedules from the 'Lydiard years' of his early career with those from his years using the Easy Interval Method below.

John van der Wansem (68) wins Dutch masters 10,000m title in 2004.
Photo: Klaas Lok

Training based on the ideas of Lydiard (1983, at age 33).

Su	17-04	Tempo 10-8-6 min, progressing in speed
Mo	18-04	Endurance run 45 min, around 3:30 per km
Tu	19-04	Tempo runs: 2x3km in 8:48, recovery 6 min jog
We	20-04	Rest
Th	21-04	Speed & coordination 6x40m increasing speed, 5x80m max speed
Fr	22-04	Fartlek 45 min, with 5x1000m to 1200m
Sa	23-04	National championships 10,000m 29:25, 2nd place

Su	18-07	Rest
Mo	19-07	Endurance run 1h, around 3:30 per km
Tu	20-07	Tempo workout progressively faster: 2x(100-300-150-300-200m), recovery 5 min jog + 2x200m max speed, recovery 400m jog
We	21-07	Endurance run 52 min, around 3:30 per km
Th	22-07	Endurance run 26 min, around 3:30 per km
Fr	23-07	Endurance run 45 min easy, 4min per km
Sa	24-07	Dutch championships 5000m 14:03

Training according to the Easy Interval Method (starting 1985, at age 35).
John van der Wansem: "In general there is not much difference in my training schedule from 1985 up until now (2006). My winter and summer training doesn't differ much. My average training is more or less the same, with the basic interval runs at a relaxed pace and the occasional harder tempos within the mixed training in the forest."

Su	Cross-country or road race
Mo	8x200m
Tu	12x200m
We	6x1000m
Th	12x200m
Fr	8x400m
Sa	Mixed training with aerobic (up to 1500m) & anaerobic tempos

John van der Wansem: "Generally, I only do the mixed training between October and April. This is because I spend most of the spring and summer racing regularly from 800m-5000m and so these races take the place of the anaerobic effect of the mixed training. If I did both a hard mixed training and a race it would place too much strain on my body and decrease my form. During such a mixed session I do surges from 50-1500m. I do not believe it is necessary to run longer distances because I regularly run road races of 10km and longer. Sometimes I would include an extra session of 6x1000m. When I got older (over 55) I only trained 5-6 times a week."

Michiel de Boer
Dutch runner, improved his 3000m time from 9:41 to 9:07 and reduced his 5000m time from 16:58 to 16:09 within six months of switching to the Easy Interval Method.

"The most important thing for me was that I have so much more fun in training since I started this method. The main reason for this is that I don't need to do any long and boring steady-state runs anymore. Another reason is that my running technique has improved a lot; I land more on my forefoot with longer strides and much better reactivity during my running! On good days I have the feeling that I am not just running but dancing. It is exactly as you have described in your book. Klaas, thank you for giving me so much more fun in running!"

Eric Borg (1967)
Top Dutch regional runner, 10km in 31:42

"I started running at age 25. I was inspired by the Olympic gold medal of Ellen van Langen in the 800m in 1992. I became a member of the local club, where I trained the usual combination of four steady-state runs and two hard interval workouts. At the beginning of 2003 I started with the Easy Interval Method. In the first month - due to the heavier load on the muscles - my legs sometimes felt 'heavy', but I was prepared, because Klaas had warned me that may happen initially. Since then I have so much more fun in running: no more boring, long steady-state runs and heavy anaerobic workouts (in the Easy Interval Method I do those just now and then). Now, nearly every workout is a positive experience. Almost sensational was the feeling of having great strength and reactivity in my legs during a race! At age of 38 I improved my time at 10km (31:42) and also ran personal bests at 3000m and 10 miles.

Apart from having more fun, I experienced the advantage of *not* having the obligation to always be training hard. Before, I just had the idea that one had to train as hard as possible in order to be able to run a good race. Remarkable also: I feel much fitter and I recover much quicker after a workout as well as after a race. For example, during my first years of running, after having done a steady-state run of 14-15km, I returned home rather languid. Now, using the same time for a workout of 6-8x1000m, I feel much better afterward. More things worth mentioning: my stride is a bit longer, I have a much better finishing kick and I regularly receive compliments about my relaxed running style. Finally and perhaps most importantly: since changing to this method I have never had any injuries!"

Carlien Harms (1968)

Dutch champion 10,000m & cross-country
Dutch record 10,000m 32:22.8, coached by Lex van Eck van der Sluijs

"During the first years of my running career I trained like so many other middle and long-distance runners: hard interval training on the track two times a week, one hill session and the rest steady-state running. It was hard for me to get used to and to believe in the Easy Interval Method of Herman Verheul. It was only thanks to my boyfriend (and later husband) Patrick Aris (5000m in 13:47), who was already a top Dutch runner and trained according to this method, that I could believe that I could run faster in races by doing most of my interval workouts easier. Also, doing none or just a few endurance runs was a bit strange too.

After only six months I started to run personal bests and from 1990-1992 I had my best years: winning Dutch titles and breaking the national record in the 10,000m with 32:22. In order to try and perform even better, I made the mistake of running my easy workouts too fast, which led to many injuries and ultimately the end of my career.

Some people may say that interval training nearly every day is boring, but I avoided this by using different routes (not always on the track) and just running using a clock. I also found a renewed strength in my legs and the actual 'running movement' felt so much better and smoother which made it even more fun!

I am convinced that many runners can benefit from this way of training. Apart from running faster race times, there are two other notable benefits: a lower chance of injury and developing a much-improved running technique in a relaxed, natural way."

Carlien Harms (409) wins Dutch cross-country title in 1992. Photo: Theo van de Rakt

Rob Boot (1960)

Dutch runner and coach

"I have been training using the Easy Interval method for some time. Only once a fortnight do I perform an easy long run of two hours – with some surges – because I run one or two marathons a year. Since changing to this method my speed has improved and I suffer fewer injuries. My best 10km time went from 46:20 down to 43:33 and I improved 10 minutes at the marathon. Klaas, thank you for your tips! For me it is clear: easy interval training is not just for top runners but also works for average runners like me who just want to improve their personal best times."

Berthold Berger (1969)

Top Dutch runner, 1500m 3:43, half marathon 1:02:29

"I started running in 1978 as a nine-year-old and, up until to my 20's, I trained according to the 'traditional' method: hard interval workouts and steady-state training, the latter mostly also fast. When I was 18-20 years old I trained harder and harder, but without satisfying results. When I reached the age of 20 this was all so frustrating that I considered quitting running altogether. In that year I struggled to realise times of 4:04 at 1500m, 8:49 at 3000m and 15:09 at 5000m.

In September 1989 I met Klaas Lok, who persuaded me to radically change my way of training. The results were astonishing: with only six workouts weekly, eight months later I ran 1500m in 3:53, 3000m in 8:17 and 5000m in 14:25. The following year these times were 3:43-8:08-14:09. I was stunned by this way of training: doing relaxed tempos like 6x1000m in 3:25 that Klaas advised me to do during the first weeks of training. Compare these to the 2:50 I used to do up to just a few weeks earlier, and compare the 10x400m in 1:15 to the 8x400m in 55-64 seconds I had done for so many years! Only once a week during certain periods I did anaerobic tempos in a mixed session in the forest, just by feel.

Note from Klaas Lok: Berthold makes a 'mistake' by comparing his 'traditional' hard tempos with the easy tempos of the Easy Interval Method. This comparison is better: the

Berthold Berger (504). Photo: Klaas Lok

traditional, steady-state training is replaced by easy interval training; the two hard, anaerobic workouts are replaced by just one mixed workout with aerobic and anaerobic tempos.

The sessions were all so incredibly slow, that in the first months I couldn't believe I would ever get any results. Then, after a couple of months, I noticed my running became more relaxed, with better strength and reactivity and I learned to run more on my forefoot. More and more I learned the exact easy interval feeling, which after about a year was so perfect that I didn't have to look at my watch to know that it was 3:20 at 1000 or 1:15 at 400m.

Also remarkable was that my energy level and running reactivity increased to a level I never had before. *(Note from Klaas Lok: This experience of Berthold matches the experience of so many runners; that they feel fitter, even after a race.)* When I was tapering off the days before a race, I had the feeling that - in a way of speaking - I was bouncing all the time. This all gave me a finishing speed that I had lost in the years before, not just to my own surprise but also to the surprise of other competitors.

The years after, from 1992-1998, I changed my focus from middle distance to road running, including marathon. I added some easy endurance runs to the Easy Interval Method: 1-2 hours, and every now and then 2.5 hours when I was preparing for a marathon. This resulted in a good time for the half marathon (1:02:29) and a reasonable 2:17:30 in my first marathon. In the year 1998 I decided to try to qualify for the World Championships. Unfortunately, I was hit by a car during a training period in Spain. This resulted in a double hernia, foot bone fractures and an Achilles injury. In the years after these caused more injuries, even an operation, and my career was over. Nowadays I am coach of my own running group, in which of course I promote the Easy Interval Method."

Bertrand Maas (1970)
Dutch 10km runner of 44:21

"During the first two years of my modest running career, I trained according to 'traditional' schedules which I found on the internet. My best performance was a 10km in 52 minutes and half marathon in two hours. For this I had to 'go very deep' and I was not happy with my performance. Therefore, I joined the running group of Berthold Berger, which uses the Easy Interval Method. My workouts immediately became more relaxed, and the easy interval training combined with a longer interval run on Sunday gave my fitness a huge boost. The next 10km race four months later was a pleasant surprise: 46:59 - five minutes faster! One week later I ran a half marathon in 1:47. Now I train three to four times a week and my personal best for 10km is 44:21."

Photo: archive Bertrand Maas

Lonneke Elzerman (1981)
Dutch 10km runner of 45:01

"I started running when I was 17 and the first 15 years I mainly did steady-state training, mostly distances from 8–15km, just once in a while longer. In those years my best time over 10km was 51:09. Unfortunately, this way of training frequently brought me injuries. After changing to the Easy Interval Method (my coach is former masters world record holder John van der Wansem) my training changed to 8–12x200m, 6x400m and almost a weekly road or cross-country race. When I don't run a race, I train 4–5x1000m.

Photo: archive Lonneke Elzerman

Within a year I noticed I got stronger and faster, resulting in a personal best of 45:01 for 10km. It is such fun to experience the increase in speed and power in my running! Also, it doesn't cost me much effort to train in this way: after around 45 minutes I am back home, satisfied and full of energy."

Russ Mullen (1986)
Haywards Heath Harriers, Sussex, UK

"I started running when I was 20 years old and initially trained using a higher mileage approach. I built up my mileage to regularly running 60–80 miles a week. I would do one or two harder interval or tempo sessions a week and on a Sunday did the traditional two-hour long run. In 2014 I managed to run 3000m in 9:35, 5000m in 16:15, 10km in 33:29 and a half marathon in 1:15:11. After reaching those times I suffered with injuries and often felt sluggish and slow. I still tried to race but never felt like I did myself justice and also didn't enjoy my training anymore. In 2016 my best times were only 10:04 for 3000m, 16:38 for 5000m, 34:17 for 10km and 1:18:24 for a half marathon. I had got slower!

In December 2016 I came across the Easy Interval Method on the internet and was intrigued. I e-mailed Klaas to find out if his book was available in English (which ultimately led me to helping him translate it). I threw away all my old training and in January 2017 I started training using the Easy Interval Method. I built up very slowly, just every other day and also running fewer repetitions. My first week was just 10x200, 8x400 and 4x1000m. Each week I added a few more reps and on Saturday I would do a local Parkrun (5km) as my anaerobic session. By March I settled on the following schedule:

Mo	15x200m
Tu	6x1000m
We	10x400m
Th	6x1000m
Fr	Rest
Sa	Parkrun (5km) or race or 8x1000m
Su	5x2km

Within a few weeks of training this way I noticed subtle changes in how I was feeling. My legs felt 'springier' and I started to feel stronger and faster. Even my old niggles and injuries started feeling better. I did my first 3000m race of the season in March 2017 and ran 9:33.15. I was amazed by this result as not only had I improved on last year's time in just a few weeks, but I'd even beaten myself from 2014. What happened after that was nothing short of amazing for me; in April I ran 5000m in 15:58 - the first time I'd ever broken 16 minutes. Over the next two months I raced nearly every weekend over distances from a mile up to 10 miles. I ran a personal best nine times in a row! My 3000m time went down to 8:59 and 5000m to 15:44. I also ran a track 10,000m in 32:55 and a road 10km in 32:51. What was most amazing was how quickly I seemed to recover from these races. I used to often need a really easy week after a race as I would be so tired, but now I had some weekends where I ran two races in two days and still ran better than I used to. The day after I ran my 10,000m personal best, I did a road 10km and ran 33:20 - still faster than my previous road best. I also had a weekend where I ran a Parkrun in 15:53 and the next day did a 5km road race in 15:45. Just six months before, either of those times would have been a massive personal best for me and now I was able to run them both one day apart.

Alongside the general positivity I should also add a caution. After six months of running the best I ever had and feeling good I slowly started declining in both fitness and health. By the end of 2017 I wasn't feeling as strong and I struggled to hit my times during sessions. My response was to try and push harder in training to hit the times I had done a couple of months prior. It seemed logical that if I replicated my sessions I would start running well again. This had disastrous results! The more I pushed the more tired and frustrated I became and the slower I raced. Throughout 2018 I struggled to reach anywhere near my performances of 2017 and gradually felt more negative about my running. It did make me question what I was doing and so I reached out to Klaas for his advice.

To Klaas it was obvious. I was over trained. I had been training far too fast relative to my fitness level for far too long. "Your 1000m times were too fast. This works for a couple of months, then the show is over. Fast may only be done in one session a week" was the matter-of-fact response. He was right. Klaas advised me to slow everything right down, accept my current fitness (which had dropped massively) and re-build slowly.

Almost immediately I felt better. I was able to complete the sessions and even found running them slower and easier far more enjoyable. I was looking forward to training again and each week I would gradually feel stronger and fitter. As we reach the end of 2018 I genuinely believe I am closing in on my PB-setting form and I have never looked forward to training as much as I do now. With a few more months of consistent 'relaxed' training I am also adamant I can go even faster!"

Silke Schmidt (1959)
Four time world champion masters 55-59 & seven world records in 2015

Her schedule during the final three weeks before her half-marathon world record.

	Week 15 Feb	Week 22 Feb	Week 1 March
Su	Am: 5x2000m Pm: 8km moderate	Am: 6x1000m Pm: 8km moderate	Race 5km in 17:36
Mo	Am: 15x200m + strength tr Pm: 8km moderate	Am: 3x(8x100m) + strength tr Pm: 8km moderate	15x200m
Tu	6x1000m	10x500m	6x1000m
We	90 min easy (around 20km; without surges)	10x400m	8x400m
Th	6x1000m	6x1000m	Warming-up
Fr	10x400m	3x(10x100m)	12x200m extra easy
Sa	Fartlek (different distances, easy & threshold speed; total distance 14 km)	Fartlek (14km)	5x400m
			Su: ½ marathon The Hague, world rec women masters 55-59 in 1h19:38

Silke Schmidt.

Photos: archive Silke Schmidt

Lex van Eck van der Sluijs, successful 'Easy-Interval Coach' for more than four decades, together with Silke Schmidt, after her World Record half marathon in March 2015.

From 1974 to 1985 I set the following personal records:

Distance	Time
100m	12.5
200m	25.6
400m	52.5
800m	1:50.3
1000m	2:21.8
1500m	3:38.8
Mile	3:57.69
2000m	5:03.9, solo run, Dutch record
3000m	7:51.4; Dutch indoor record
5000m	13:36.1
10,000m	28:24.7, solo run
15km	44:19
20km	59:30

In the beginning I trained hard

I first started running as a 16-year-old and initially did little more than a 5km training run once a week. I ran this as fast as possible with my main goal being the annual local village run. I was very active as a teenager and built my aerobic base with six years of cycling to and from high school. I totalled about 36km a day and would mostly ride as fast as I could. I only started running seriously when I was 18 and began with 2-3 sessions per week. This would always be a 5-8km run as fast as I could manage. I'd always try and sprint the last 400m. After five months of this training (and the two years of irregular running once a week before) I managed to run a 10km road race in 34 minutes. This inspired me to join a track club in a neighbouring city and three days later I ran my first ever track race - 5000m in 15:56. The coach at this club was a former runner, without any serious knowledge about coaching, and the only thing he knew was to 'train hard'! So I increased my training to four times a week and apart from the two hard endurance runs of 8km, I added two anaerobic sessions such as 10x200m in 28 seconds or 4x400m in 62-64 seconds. By the end of that track season I ran 3000m in 9:20, 1500m in 4:17 and 800m in 2:00.4.

The change to easy interval training

At the end of the summer I started my university studies and moved to Utrecht. That winter I joined a local club, Phoenix, and met Herman Verheul. Under his guidance I changed my training to the Easy Interval Method and ran six sessions per week. These included 15x200m in 34 seconds, 10x400m in 75 seconds (sometimes twice a week), 6x1000m in 3:25-3:30 (again, twice a week) and one cross-country race. If I didn't race I would do another session of 6x1000m. Other than a few strides after warming up I did no real speed work and no anaerobic training - this would come a year later.

To begin with I was very sceptical. I wasn't convinced I could run faster without training faster or harder, but my new running mates assured me that if I was patient I would reap the rewards. They echoed my concerns but said after they started running personal bests that their doubts were eased and they started believing in the training.

Their promise held true and after two months of this new kind of training I improved my 800m personal best by running 1:57 in an indoor race. I was stunned and surprised that I could run a three-second personal best without any hard training. My confidence and belief in the training had increased dramatically!

The following tables are actual schedules of my training at various points of my running career. Every session - even the endurance runs with surges - began with a 10-15 minute warm-up jog and some exercises like mild stretching, core stability, hopping and bounding (Verheul was the first in the Netherlands to introduce all kind of exercises). All sessions were done with a brief walk before and after the harder effort followed by a recovery jog as described in chapter 6. I would always conclude my warm-up with 3-4 strides of about 80m before starting my session. My cool-down was generally no more than a 10-minute jog.

Klaas Lok leading during a 5000m in Brussels, 1974. Lok ran a Dutch junior record in 14:25 His teammate Ad Buijs runs in 2nd position. Photo: Theo van de Rakt

Track season 1974, as a 19-year-old.

Mo	10x400m 1:15-1:13
Tu	6x1000m 3:25-3:20
We	15x200m 34-33
Th	6x1000m 3:25-3:20
Fr	10x400m 1:15-1:10
Sa	Rest
Su	Track race 3000m 8:45

Track season, June 1976, as a 21-year-old

In the final week before national championships 1500m I skipped the 1000m's.

	Week 1	Week 2
Su	Race 3000m 8:07	Race 1500m 3:47.5
Mo	10x400m 1:14	15x200m 32-31
Tu	6x1000m 3:15-3:10	6x1000m 3:15
We	15x200m 32-31 (sometimes 30.5)	10x400m 1:12-1:10
Th	10x400m 1:15	14x200m 32, 1x200m 28
Fr	Track race 800m 1:53	Rest
Sa	6x1000m 3:20	10x200m in 36
		Su: Race 1500m 3:42.3

Cross-country season, January 1978, as a 23-year-old

Extending 6x1000 to 8x1000m improved my aerobic endurance.

Mo	Am: 6x1000m 3:30; pm: gym work (extra weekly 1 hr gym workout in winter: core stability, dynamic stretching, bouncing, etc)
Tu	8x1000m 3:20
We	15x200m 34
Th	8x1000m 3:20
Fr	10x400m 1:14
Sa	Mixed training in forest: exercises, speed, hills, aerobic and anaerobic tempos
Su	Cross-country race, around 10km

Indoor season March 1978, as a 23-year-old

Tapering before European Indoor Championships in Italy in 1978.

Sa	Mixed session in forest: exercises, speed, hills, aerobic and anaerobic tempos
Su	6x1000m easy 3:15
Mo	Rest
Tu	6x1000m easy 3:15
We	15x200m easy 32
Th	6x400m easy 1:13-1:14
Fr	3x400m easy 1:14 (scheduled heats 3000m at Saturday were unexpectedly canceled, else I would have trained a bit more at Thursday and Friday)
Sa	2x400m easy 1:14
Su	3000m EC indoor, 5th in 7:51.4, personal best by five seconds and Dutch record

Results European Indoor Championships 1978

1	Markus Ryffel	Switzerland	7:49.5
2	Emiel Puttemans	Belgium	7:49.9
3	Jörg Peter	East Germany	7:50.1
4	Dan Glans	Sweden	7:51.2
5	Klaas Lok	Netherlands	7:51.4
6	Karl Fleschen	West Germany	7:53.9
7	Paul Thijs	Belgium	7:55.7
8	Venanzio Ortis	Italy	7:55.8
9	Józef Ziubrak	Poland	7:56.2
10	Dietmar Millonig	Austria	7:57.5
11	Christian Sanjurjo	Spain	7:58.1
12	Patriz Ilg	West Germany	7:58.8
13	Ari Paunonen	Finland	8:07.3
14	Ingo Sensburg	West Germany	8:12.5

End of January 1979, as a 24-year-old

At the end of February 1979, I won my first of six Dutch cross-country titles. Due to an injury I couldn't perform the mixed training in the forest and neither my 200m session. I noticed the 2000m's gave me better aerobic endurance, although those were originally not present in the Easy Interval Method.

Mo	Am: 8x1000m 3:30; pm: 1 hr gymnastic
Tu	5x2000m 7:00 mins (1 month later: 6:45-6:40)
We	10x400m 1:16 (1 month later 1:12)
Th	8x1000m 3:20 (1 month later 3:10)
Fr	5x2000m 7:00
Sa	10x400m 1:15
Su	8x1000m 3:20

Training camp in Italy, April 1979, as a 24-year-old

The extra morning sessions gave me better stamina at 10km. In the first seven days, during 10 workouts, I ran 71km at speeds of 17.1 km/h to 23.6 km/h, including 10 workouts worth of 3x80m strides, which were faster than 24km/h, all in a relaxed way. In my view that is quality, specific mileage… An interesting exercise for you: add up the total volume of 'quality' (just under marathon pace up to 1500 or 800m pace) miles you do throughout the week.

Klaas Lok wins the first of his six Dutch cross-country titles in 1979, against tough competition from Gerard Nijboer (no 482 - 1980 Olympic marathon silver winner) and Gerard Tebroke (no 494 - former Dutch record holder 5000m (13:21) and 10,000m (27:36). Photo: Theo van de Rakt

	Week 1	Week 2
Fr	8x1000m 3:15-3:10	10x400m 1:10-1:08
Sa	Am: 7km w surges; basic speed 3:30/km Pm: 15 x200m 31	8x1000m 3:08-3:04
Su	5x2000m 6:45-6:40	Am: 7km w surges (same as before) Pm: 15x200m in 31-30.5
Mo	Am: 7km w surges (same as before) Pm: 10x400m 1:11-1:09	Rest, travel back to Holland
Tu	8x1000m 3:10-3:05	15x200m 32
We	Am: 7km w surges (same as before) Pm: 15x200 m 31-30.5	10x400m 74
Th	5x2000m 6:40-6:35	10x400 m 1:16
		Fr: 10,000m, solo run in 28:24.7

Schedule in February 1980, as a 25-year-old

The 10km morning runs gave me stamina for cross-country races, but made me slower over 800 and 1500m. From this I learned: no endurance runs for 800 & 1500m runners in track season, and also none for 5000m runners in the final two weeks before a peak race.

Mo	Am: 5x2000m 6:50 Pm: 1 hr gymnastics
Tu	Am: moderate fast 10km run in 36 mins, w surges of 1 minute Pm: 6x1000m 3:15
We	Am: same 10km run as Tu Pm: 15x200m 34-33
Th	6x1000m 3:15-3:10
Fr	8x400m 1:15-1:13
Sa	Mixed training, relaxed
Su	Dutch cross-country Championships 12km, my 2nd national cross title

Later I experimented with faster endurance runs with surges, as fast as 33 minutes over 10km. However, this was a huge mistake: combined with the races it was too intense. This was one of the mistakes I made. Another mistake was that during a busy track season I would run the 1000m sessions too fast, which sometimes caused loss of form.

In 1981 I completely changed my training and experimented with the 'traditional approach', but that didn't go well, as I will explain in chapter 5.1.

4. Lactate threshold - Science supporting easy interval training

I would like to express my thanks and gratitude to Dr Eugene Janssen, Dutch sports physiologist and Adri Hartveld, physiotherapist and distance runner, for their help in writing the following chapter.

Lactate threshold

Most people believe that there is a clear dividing line between the anaerobic (without oxygen) and aerobic (with oxygen) energy systems when we are running. It is widely believed that at slower, relaxed speeds we are using our aerobic system and then at faster speeds our bodies switch to using our anaerobic system. In reality, however, all systems are always active but the degree to which each is being used varies depending on the intensity of the effort. These energy systems include the aerobic fat burning, aerobic carbohydrate combustion, anaerobic carbohydrate burning (with lactic acid accumulation) and the alactic anaerobic energy system (without lactic acid accumulation).

During moderate intensity exercise, energy can be supplied with minimal acidification - which is caused by the production of hydrogen ions ($H+$; an ion is an electrically charged particle). At the easier paces that are used for a longer, sustained effort, energy is mainly released from the aerobic energy supply.

During high-intensity exercise the aerobic system is still functioning, but it is unable to produce energy fast enough to match the requirements the muscles demand. This results in our bodies switching to our anaerobic system, which does not require oxygen to produce energy. However, the anaerobic pathway also produces a by-product called lactic acid, which you will probably know as the painful feeling you get during hard efforts. It is often blamed for fatigue, muscle soreness and every other negative feeling associated with training and racing.

However, lactic acid doesn't really exist in the body for long. It dissipates very quickly - almost as soon as it's formed it is split into lactate and acid ($H+$). Lactate is actually our friend, not a foe. It can be used by the muscles, brain and heart and also be put through what's known as the 'lactate shuffle' in the liver, which converts it to glucose - another highly useful fuel source! Highly-trained athletes are capable of using vast amounts of lactate to fuel their muscles. They also have high amounts of transporter enzymes to get the lactate out of the blood and back into the muscles where it can be 'burned' for fuel.

The negative effect of this process is that, while it provides the quick energy that the runner requires, the hydrogen ions ($H+$) which are split off can build up, causing an acidic environment in the muscles, which impairs their function and forces them to slow down. This is the feeling you get when your muscles seize up and you feel short of breath. The body has natural buffering mechanisms in place to deal with this build-up and again, this can be improved with training.

The point at which the body switches from predominantly aerobic to predominantly anaerobic energy is highly dependent on fitness and this point is often referred to as your lactate threshold. There is a point, during increased intensity exercise, that an individual will show rapidly increased levels of blood lactate. This turning point is referred to as the 'Onset of Blood Lactate Accumulation' or OBLA. The OBLA is considered to correspond with the Lactate Threshold as the point where the balance between the production of lactate and the speed of its removal has been passed. This means that your body is producing too much lactate (and the resulting hydrogen ions) for it to clear, which results in your muscles having to slow down.

The concept of a threshold - where we switch over from predominately aerobic to anaerobic energy - is an important one. Training around - and especially under - this intensity is a very effective and efficient way to improve fitness and form. Research has shown that intensity just under the lactate threshold produces the highest values of lactate clearance, up to 30% more than at or above the threshold. Obviously, it is this 'clearing system' that we want to be as good as possible and it is not a coincidence that the training paces of the longer, basic interval sessions (over about two minutes) in the Easy Interval Method are performed under the threshold pace most of the time. Training above the lactate threshold does have its place of course, but to a much smaller extent than many runners would believe. Too much training above this threshold places a huge strain on the body and muscles and can lead to overtraining.

The 'threshold training effect' also explains why it doesn't always mean that doing sessions considerably faster than your race pace results in faster race times. If you run your sessions too fast you will be training far beyond your threshold and so will be training yourself to use your anaerobic energy system while neglecting your more economical aerobic system. Bear in mind that even shorter races (1500m) are fundamentally aerobic events (over 70% of your energy will be aerobic), so the bulk of your training should be under the lactate threshold. The longer the event, the more the aerobic system is the dominant force. The Easy Interval Method means you can train close to your threshold several times a week without breaking down and, therefore, slowly increase your body's lactate threshold.

How to determine your anaerobic threshold

Across the general population the lactate threshold is highly individual and a designated point is hard to calculate. This is why the athlete must be very careful when training near the threshold and why I always make a very important point when doing an Easy Interval Session: *it's better to be 10 seconds per 1000m too slow than one second too fast!*

You can roughly work out your lactate threshold pace from the distance you can run in 45-60 minutes race effort. For moderately fast runners this will be around 10-15km race pace. For an elite runner this will be more like their half-marathon race pace, while it might be 7-8km for slower runners. You should also be aware that your threshold pace can vary every day, depending on many other factors. Fatigue after a race or hard effort, lack of sleep, bad nutrition, bad weather: so many things can affect how your body performs. You must learn to feel how your body is coping with each training session, which is why all aerobic repetitions over two minutes must be well below the threshold. It is very easy for a runner to train too fast, thinking they are superman, only for their body to bite back after three or four repetitions as the session becomes too hard.

The following paragraphs are meant for those runners who are experienced in using a heart-rate monitor and know they can rely on the obtained information. Others, who like to keep things simple, can skip this part *(don't worry, the guidelines and table in chapter 6 will give you good starting points for the speed of your easy intervals)* and jump to the paragraphs about muscle fibre types on page 37. They should only keep in mind the following intensity zones: easy endurance run (zone 1), moderate endurance run (zone 2), fast endurance run (zone 3) and tempo (zone 4).

Deriving your anaerobic threshold from a 30-minute time trial

Rather than using a race pace to determine your threshold, a 30-minute time trial could be even more accurate. Taken from the website training4endurance.co.uk:

"An important consideration is that during race situations heart rates tend to be elevated due to increased adrenaline levels which can alter the heart rate-threshold relationship. For example, it could be 175 while running a 45-60 minute race, opposed to 172 in training conditions. So, for most people, training at the heart rate achieved in race situations would result in lactate values in excess of the lactate threshold. A better option is to undertake a 30-minute time trial in a non-competitive situation whilst recording the heart rate throughout. Research has found the 30-minute time trial method to be a good predictor of velocity and heart rate at the lactate threshold (McGehee et al., 2005). To use this method complete a 30-minute time trial and record your heart rate over the last 20 minutes. Calculate your average heart rate over your last 20 minutes and average your speed, or power, over the time trial. Your average speed/power and heart rate should equate - to a reasonable level of accuracy - with your lactate threshold."

There are mathematical ways of estimating your heart rate at your lactate threshold pace as well, but I should stress these are not considered 100% accurate. The simplest one is: lactate threshold heart rate is approximately 85-90% of maximum heart rate, although it could be 80-85% or even 93% in some individuals.

As mentioned previously, heart rate can fluctuate on a daily basis and so is not deemed to be an accurate measure of an athlete's threshold.

Three main groups of aerobic steady-state run intensity

Traditionally, steady-state runs are divided into the following three groups: easy endurance run (also named zone 1), moderate endurance run (zone 2) and fast endurance run (zone 3). I should point out that this only applies to athletes who are capable of a clear difference in training speed. Unfortunately, some - especially slower - runners are stuck into one speed and it doesn't make much difference whether they are running a 5km or a marathon, they still travel at the same pace. This is often a result of very poor reactivity and power in their muscles and so as soon as they try to run quickly, they immediately cross over their lactate threshold and into their anaerobic zone. Also, the percentages mentioned hereafter are not accurate for slower and poorly trained runners.

Easy endurance run (zone 1)

According to the general consensus, an easy endurance run is performed at about 75-80% of lactate threshold effort. For decades it was widely believed that long, slow endurance training promotes a more efficient use of fat as a fuel (used for weight loss) alongside utilising carbohydrate. Easy endurance runs also improve the hormone and enzyme action, as well as the energy stores (glycogen) in the muscles and liver. The slow-twitch muscle fibres are dominantly trained in this zone.

Experience has taught us, however, that these slow endurance runs do not have to be part of a training program for distances up to a half marathon. When you train according to the Easy Interval Method the same effects can be achieved with long, relatively slow (and therefore aerobic) intervals along with long recovery breaks. I realise that some runners enjoy the long, slower runs but I would urge you to implement some surges to break up the monotony and constant slower speed. I am not against the positive effects that can be obtained from longer, slower runs, but I am against the monotonous, continuous character of it, which has a negative effect on your muscles' ability to run quickly and therefore damages your running economy. If you spend 60 minutes running very slowly you will have trained your aerobic system, but you will have also trained your muscles to move very slowly.

Modern studies show that interval training actually burns more fat than longer, slower running and also creates the so-called 'after burn' effect where your body continues to burn fat after you have finished exercising.

Moderate endurance run (zone 2)

This is an endurance run at a medium pace or around 85-90% of your lactate threshold intensity. Moderate endurance training enhances aerobic metabolism, the heart-lung, blood circulation and energy conversion of carbohydrates to the muscles, blood flow to the muscles, enzyme activity, the anaerobic threshold and the energy store in muscles. You will achieve the same effects in the Easy Interval Method when you run relaxed intervals of 1000-2000m (in combination with the long rests in between the intervals) and moderate endurance runs with surges.

Fast endurance run (zone 3)

The fast aerobic endurance run is performed at roughly 90-95% of the lactate threshold. These runs are key to raising your threshold to new levels and increase your oxygen uptake. They train your body to better process and remove the lactate waste product (H+ ions). However, the caveat is that for many runners performing such runs of 30-40 minutes several times a week is too taxing. That is why training at this intensity in the Easy Interval Method will involve just occasional fast endurance runs with surges, but regularly performing easy intervals over various distances. For example, by performing aerobic 1000m intervals we have the advantage of being able to regularly stress the intensity around 90-95% of the lactate threshold intensity without the taxing effort of longer runs.

Jogging and tempo (zone 0 & 4)

Alongside the aforementioned paces I will also use the terms jogging and tempo. Jogging (could be named zone 0) is clear to everybody. Tempo (zone 4) is around anaerobic threshold, which for faster runners - in training - will feel similar to 10km race intensity and for slower runners closer to 5km intensity. I emphasise that in training it will generally be slower than their race *pace*.

With regard to aerobic training, in the Easy Interval Method we mainly focus on zone 2 and zone 3, and scarcely run faster than lactate threshold (LT) intensity. Zone 1 will automatically be stressed during warming up and the active rests during interval training. Be aware that - when aiming for an aerobic workout - you should not reach the higher intensity (above 92% of LT) when performing longer intervals, such as 2000m. Please note that all the aforementioned intensities apply to aerobic workouts. Hard, anaerobic training will be discussed further on. I should also point out that for the shorter easy intervals (200-400m) you will be running above your threshold pace. However, these are much shorter intervals and along with the longer recover breaks, they cannot be considered anaerobic training.

Runners who like to use a heart rate monitor might be interested in using the so called Zoladz-test, developed by the Polish physiologist Professor Jerzy Zoladz. This test is quite simple, easy to apply (run 5x6 minutes at five different heart rates), and it gives a reasonably clear picture of your fitness at various effort zones. You can find it on the internet. Please note that the Zoladz-zones should be used for testing only, because they are averages and not necessarily the same as your personal effort zones.

Muscle fibre types

Muscles fibres can be divided into two distinct types: slow-twitch (type 1) and fast-twitch (type 2). Slow-twitch muscle fibres are mainly used in relatively slow endurance activities in which the aerobic energy supply is dominant. They can sustain - after adequate training - such an effort for several hours. Fast-twitch muscle fibres (type 2) are mainly used in higher speed activities, with a much higher use of anaerobic energy. The flipside is that type 2 fibres fatigue quicker. On average, untrained people have a ratio of about 50:50 between type 1 and 2 fibres in their prime moving muscles. Top long-distance runners, however, have a much higher percentage (around 80%) of slow-twitch fibres, while in top sprinters it is the other way around.

It is generally accepted that fast-twitch fibres (type 2) can be further categorized into type 2c, 2a and type 2b (also named 2x) fibres. (Some researchers divide even further, obtaining a total of 6-7 types.) Type 2b functions purely anaerobically without producing lactic acid. Type 2a also functions anaerobically but produces lactic acid. Fast twitch 2c fibres are known as intermediate, and are actually a combination of type 1 and type 2 muscle fibers. Type 2c can use both aerobic and anaerobic energy. Due to their aerobic characteristics, type 2c fibres can sustain an effort longer than type 2b and 2a, but not as long as type 1.

It is important and beneficial to train the aerobic function of the fast twitch fibre type 2 more than is done in conventional training programmes and the Easy Interval Method achieves this by stimulating both the fast and slow twitch fibres in every session.

When you run a race you will always recruit a mix of fibre types. So, training all muscle fibre types will benefit your race times considerably, plus it will give you a much better finishing kick. However, in order to avoid exhausting the 'vulnerable' type 2c fibres, these fibres should not be stressed with too many fast distance runs in zone 3 intensity, but in a light way, e.g. through performing easy 1000m intervals, with long active rests (as will be discussed in chapter 6).

No more than one hard session a week

Scientific research supports my opinion (and my experience) that, for most runners, just one heavy session a week - and the rest light - is the best and safest way to improve. In the following paragraphs I summarize a study by former top Dutch runner Adri Hartveld. He finished 5th in the Dutch Cross Country Championships in 1984 (see photo in chapter 8.6) and won the Dutch marathon title in 1986. He has worked as a physiotherapist in the UK since 1982 and, during that time, has assessed hundreds of runners with overuse injuries. As part of the assessment Adri looked at both the athletes' biomechanics and their training history. Adri also researched various training ideas and methodologies, including Easy Interval training.

When you stress your body in a training session, muscle protein will break down. This needs to build up again (muscle protein synthesis). Research has shown that this will take around a week or so after you did a hard session (or a race). Next you will have reached super-compensation. However, to achieve the best super-compensation, you should not rest completely. A few lighter sessions in that week of recovery aids in this super-compensation process. How many, and their intensity, will depend on how well-trained you are. When you do this in the correct way, after a week you will not only have better stamina, but your muscles and tendons will be less prone to injuries.

The intensity of the lighter sessions should not be too low, so preferably not slow steady runs. And adding another hard training session too soon will result in the body breaking down instead of achieving super-compensation. Easy interval sessions, however, ensure that the total muscle protein synthesis is greater than the muscle protein breakdown at every microcycle of training. The Easy Interval Method provides this balanced training with the right intensity and volume needed to make sure the athlete builds up rather than breaks down.

The graph below shows the recovery of an athlete training every day. Starting with a hard session on day 1, the following six days are lighter sessions. Another heavy session is performed on day 8. In this way there will be more muscle protein synthesis than muscle protein breakdown, which results in super-compensation.

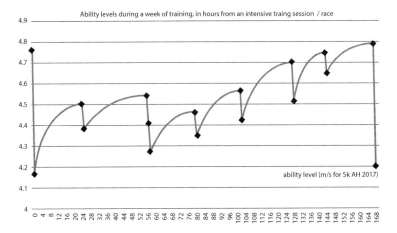

Read the complete article by Adri Hartveld on easyintervalmethod.com.

In chapter 5 you will find some more research supporting the power and efficiency of the Easy Interval Method.

5. Aerobic, anaerobic and the importance of reactivity

In this chapter I will make clear why the relatively light Easy Interval Method of Verheul can work better for most runners compared to the more traditional higher mileage, steady-state running approach that is more commonly practiced by most of the world's runners. I will discuss steady-state training, anaerobic training, reactivity and finally give some advice for young and novice runners.

5.1   Aerobic training: not steady pace but interval based

It is a widely accepted opinion that steady-state running should be the basis of all distance runners' programmes. Nearly every schedule on the internet or in books will claim that all runners should do at least 70% of their training at a low intensity, steady-state range. This is based on the opinion that physiological evidence shows that slow endurance training improves the aerobic ability of the muscles and that many world class athletes have included incredibly high volumes of slower endurance training in their schedule.

Unfortunately, many coaches and athletes choose to neglect (or even accept) the negative effects of a lot of repetitive, slower and steady-state training - increased risk of injury, deterioration of muscle reactivity (running economy) and reduction of speed. It is worth noting that even the legendary coach Arthur Lydiard - whose name has become synonymous with 160km weeks - realised the risk of losing reactivity and speed. This was the reason why he insisted his athletes followed up the 'long as possible' base phase of steady mileage with a hill phase. This involved bounding and striding up very steep hills and very fast downhill 'over-speed' runs with the goal of putting the zip and spring back into the legs before doing the more specific track work required to run fast races. Lydiard's most famous athlete, the great Peter Snell, said that if he could go back and change one thing about his training, he would have included a weekly session of 400m repeats (even during his base phase) just to keep the spring and speed in his legs. He always said he found it very hard to run fast after his high mileage build up.

Mistakes regarding steady-state training

Unfortunately, many runners who follow Lydiard's ideas do not understand them fully. His system was very complex and all phases were equally as important, but names such as 'the father of jogging' have given the impression that his entire training philosophy is based on huge amounts of slower, steady running. Many runners incorrectly get stuck into the mind-set that by running loads of slower, steady miles they are interpreting Lydiard's ideas. However, it is a widely spread misconception that his base phase was just slow endurance running. Firstly, in this base phase he also let his athletes perform fartleks, in which tempos from 30 seconds up to 5 minutes were run with long recoveries between the repeats. The paces of the faster parts were anywhere from 5km to half-marathon pace, not by the clock but more by feel. Secondly, the endurance runs were not slow, steady runs, but mostly fast and performed in a hilly environment, which made them actually more akin aerobic interval training!

Physiologist Hans Keizer, former national coach and team physician of the Dutch Athletic Union, once told me how easily the 'Lydiard-approach' can be misinterpreted. In the winter of 1968-1969 Arthur Lydiard gave a lecture in the Netherlands in which he talked about his high mileage, low intensity endurance training for middle distance runners. Several top Dutch runners followed suit, including Keizer's wife, Ilja Keizer-Laman (6th in the Olympic 1500m in 1972 – pb 4:05). All runners performed worse in 1969 with the only minor success coming at the end of that track season where some runners managed to equal their performances of the year before. Dr Hans Keizer: "Only later we learned that Lydiard's endurance runs were actually high-end aerobic interval runs of 800m up-hill with a recovery run back down. Due to the flat environment in the Netherlands, for us it became a steady slow run with no variation in intensity. When you do slow, steady state training, you will 'untrain' your fast type 2 muscle fibers".

Later in his career, Keizer regularly tested several elite runners in his lab at the University of Utrecht. This was done on a treadmill with continuous monitoring of ventilation. He found that at submaximal intensities the caloric cost of running increased after too much slow endurance training. Thus, running efficiency decreased with this type of slow training. This situation disappeared after the training intensity was increased. After a careful study of the training schedules of these runners he found that in order to improve performance, training volume is less important than intensity (nowadays proven by scientific studies), on condition that the latter was done in a relaxed way. Thereafter his credo was: "Train as least and light as possible to improve". He emphasises that a coach should always analyse which type of muscle fibres are predominantly activated during a certain race distance.

He applied his findings by letting his athletes perform short but fast aerobic runs of 10-15 minutes. He also found that a tapering phase can be up to two weeks without losing form, as long as - especially for middle distance runners - the fast twitch 2 fibres are used in a lighter way of training. Hans Keizer: "Extensive interval training as described in this book comes close to my ideas of how to build aerobic endurance."

It is worth noting that Lydiard's base phase was first followed by a hill training phase and next a racing phase which included up to six interval sessions a week! Unfortunately, many middle distance runners nowadays get scared of skipping their steady-state training, even during racing periods. They may well do two interval sessions a week but, unfortunately for them, much more speed training is required to compensate the loss of reactivity and efficacy of the fast twitch fibres from the steady base period. Many elite runners can overcome this because they train up to 12 times per week (often with fast endurance runs and many interval sessions). They also have the benefit of being able to rest more and have access to regular massages and physiotherapists to avoid injuries. For an everyday athlete this is really not possible, and so in this book I am going to share with you a way you can train less but still increase and enhance your aerobic power, alongside maintaining and developing your personal reactivity and running economy.

Train your aerobic power while not losing running economy - even improve it!

Perhaps the most interesting aspect of the Easy Interval Method is the emphasis on 'muscle reactivity' and running economy. Many coaches and athletes see distance running purely from an aerobic point of view and ignore how our muscles actually react and move at speed. If you want to see a great example of this in action, watch some slow-motion videos of elite Kenyan or Ethiopian runners. Almost as soon as their feet strike the ground, they 'bounce' back into flight. Their muscles, tendons and ligaments are so strong and 'reactive' that they literally recoil off the ground. This is referred to as 'elastic energy' by physiologists and biomechanists and is essentially 'free' energy supplied upon landing. For a real-world example imagine dropping two golf balls from the same height with one landing on concrete and another on grass. The ball landing on the concrete will bounce higher, even though the energy supplied is the same, due to the harder surface and greater 'elastic energy' the ball can get from the ground. A truly elite runner runs in a similar way, using as much 'elastic energy' as possible during each foot strike. It is a natural version of the incredible spring return that the amazing amputee runners get from their carbon-fibre blades.

Running economy does matter, some scientific research

Research from the former Olympic champion Dr Peter Snell, during the 1980s, found that runners who completed a twice weekly session of 200 or 400m intervals at a moderate pace (very similar to the 200 and 400m intervals in the Easy Interval Method), improved on average by a minute over a 10km distance when compared with a control group. The control group performed a rapid endurance run of 29 minutes in place of the intervals. All other sessions were the same for both groups and consisted of slow and moderate endurance runs. The results showed that maximum oxygen uptake (VO2max) was better developed in the interval group. Another conclusion was that, due to training at closer to race pace, the interval trained runners were more economical at their desired race speed compared to the control group. It is now widely accepted that running economy improves the most at the speed the runner practices the most. For example, a runner who spends 30% of their training running at 10km pace will be more economical at that speed than a runner who only spends 10% of their training at that pace. Yet, surprisingly, so many runners still mainly do steady-state runs for the vast majority of all their training.

From the website pponline.co.uk: "Finnish researcher Laina Paavolainen provided strong evidence that workouts which combine high-speed running intervals with explosive strengthening movements (hops, jumps, bounds, etc) can significantly improve 5km race times. In this study, runners who increased mileage from 70km to 110km per week failed to improve 5km times, while runners who remained at 70km but added explosive running and strength drills to their training bettered their 5km performances by around 30 seconds. The explosively trained runners improved running economy and overall power, while the 110km runners were unable to do so."

World-class runners and slow endurance training

However, what about world class runners, such as the great Haile Gebreselassie, multiple Olympic champion who also broke 27 world records from 2000m indoor up to the marathon? He said that long, relatively slow endurance running is at the heart of his training and that these runs allow his body to increase its ability to absorb oxygen. Of course, without question, slow aerobic distance training has positive effects and you will find longer runs are easier to accomplish. When training for very long distances like a marathon they are an important part of training. However, long runs can still be done with surges and changes in pace and I would urge you to implement these if training for a longer race.

The problem starts when there is no balance in the training between the fast and slower mileage. You may well increase your aerobic ability and your body's ability to absorb oxygen which, theoretically, might take off one minute from your 10km time. However, you may also lose your reactive style of running, natural speed and efficacy of your fast twitch fibres which may make you two minutes slower. Thus, your actual performance is worse! With so many steady-state runs as your basic training you will have to do a lot of extra, faster miles to compensate for this and restore your lost running economy. This is one of the advantages of the Easy Interval Method: there is no need to do these 'compensation miles'.

For Haile the slow, steady run is at the heart of his aerobic training, but in the Easy Interval Method the heart consists of the relaxed 1000m intervals (sometimes 2000m for advanced runners): 1000m fast, 800m recovery at an easy pace repeated 4, 6 and maybe even 10 times for a well-trained athlete. In this way you have the advantage of easy endurance training but not the disadvantages of the slow, monotone running. Essentially, you are training your aerobic system as well as your economy and reactivity at the same time.

World-class runners and their reactivity

Why then do so many elite runners run world records and win Olympic medals with traditional methods in which they have 6-7 endurance runs per week? Why is their natural reactivity - as well as their fast twitch 2 fibres - not killed off by all their steady-state training?

I suggest the main reasons for this might include:
• Volume (already mentioned in this chapter): they do a lot of fast interval training which compensates for all the slow endurance runs. It was observed that these elite runners train at a greater proportion of their weekly mileage around 10km race speed.

- Being born with a superior natural reactivity and carrying less weight than the average runner (for many world-class runners this is less than 60kg; marathon world record holder of 2018, Eliud Kipchoge, weighs just 52kg). With a low weight it is easier to maintain a reactive running style, even when doing endurance runs.

I myself was 64kg and after a successful seven years training under Verheul and the Easy Interval Method I changed my training schedule and experimented with 2-3 long, slow (60-90 minutes) endurance runs a week. I was reliably assured by a respected coach that, within two months, I should be able to run under 28 minutes over 10km because "I would benefit quickly from the long aerobic runs". The reality, however, was shocking. My reactivity went down to the level of a recreational runner, my 10km time slowed by a minute and my finishing speed of 54-56 seconds over the last 400m was reduced to 58! My new coach, who prescribed me long runs, had forgotten to compensate all these slower miles with lots of reactivity and speed training. After this experiment over four months I went back to my former training and regained my old form.

Another example: a former Dutch athlete (30 minutes for 10km) mentioned to me that once, after a period of *not* training, he was able to run the 100m one second faster than after a period of heavy endurance training. This is a good example of a runner not having the correct balance in his training. So, a heavy endurance schedule may enhance your aerobic ability, but it will most likely also suppress and reduce your speed and reactivity.

It is clear to me that reactivity and running economy are incredibly important in distance running performance. This is why many physiologists recommend plyometric exercises (explosive jumps and hops) to increase performance. However, these exercises are stressful and carry a high risk of injury, especially if one does not build up to them. Much safer - and more enjoyable for most runners - is to do 3-4 sprints (or strides) at gradually increasing speeds of 80-100m after warming up. You will also benefit greatly from running 3-5x100m (some runners can go up to 10x100m) twice a week before or after your normal sessions, on top of your usual 3-4 warm-up strides. Try to run these 100m repeats at about 800-1500m race pace (start at 1500m and gradually get faster). As a distance runner you will use more strength to run these speeds and so it is a very specific strength workout. Occasionally, you can even do an entire session of 15-25x100m. These 100m's are also useful to do in a recovery period to get your legs used to running quickly again. However, there can be an injury risk: if you are not well-trained or not yet used to interval training, take a year or more to gradually implement them into your training. If you suddenly jump into 20x100m and you are not used to it, you may have heavy legs for a number of days after! In the schedules I often add these notes alongside the main session (such as 6x1000m + 3-5x100m). There is no set time when you choose to perform these extra 100's; some runners prefer to do them at the start of their session, whilst others at the end. By default I list 3-5x100m, but when starting I would suggest you just try two.

Maintain your reactivity all year round

In contrast with the Lydiard Method, in which endurance training is applied in the first aerobic phase of training, the Easy Interval Method is designed to build and maintain 'reactivity' while building an aerobic base. You don't need to do a specific hill phase and then an anaerobic phase before you are ready to race. You never flatten your basic speed, but instead are working on developing the neuro-muscular connections you need to run fast - and increasing your running economy in an efficient way - all year round.

The well-known British coach Frank Horwill also opposed the high mileage training of Lydiard. He was in favour of doing a lot of interval training at five different paces around race speed and maintaining speed and reactivity all year round. He developed this system in the early 1970s (years after Verheul started his Easy Interval Method). This 5-Tier System was also adopted by double Olympic champion and multiple world record holder Sebastian Coe.

Many runners are scared of not doing steady-state runs in race weeks

I mentioned previously how many middle-distance runners (800-5000m), who do their steady-state training in their aerobic base phase, continue to do these runs during racing periods. They are afraid of losing their aerobic endurance and feel that the only way to maintain it is to continue with the long, steady runs. They also do not have an alternative for recovery training between races and so they have another reason for their slow runs. This actually increases their risk of injury but also runs the risk of reducing and blunting their finishing speed and running economy in their peak race season. For a younger athlete - who is still training at low mileage - this doesn't have too much of an effect and their first year of racing goes well, but gradually their slow mileage increases, causing their running economy to deteriorate as the years go by.

Even some elite runners suffer from steady-state training

It is worth noting that only a very small percentage of runners in the world actually perform well with a lot of steady-state training. Most athletes who train very high mileage actually perform much better with a lighter, smarter schedule. I recall a former top Dutch 800m runner telling me that due to extra steady-state training his aerobic endurance was better than ever as he tried to regain his peak form (when he used to train only six times a week with many intervals). He was excited for his season ahead with his new fitness but unfortunately the result was his worst year ever.

Bram Som (218) and Arnoud Okken experienced the disadvantages of steady state training. Photo: Klaas Lok

Similar experiences were had by 2006 European 800m champion Bram Som and 2007 European indoor 800m champion Arnoud Okken. Both were coached by a higher mileage advocate. Gradually the running style of both athletes deteriorated which resulted in slower performances and injuries. More detail of this in the 800m chapter, where you can find a comparison of an old schedule (which was more like a 10km schedule) and a new schedule (based on easy interval training) of Bram Som.

No recovery steady-state runs in the Easy Interval Method
Many middle-distance runners use so called 'easy recovery runs' in their training plans. But can we really call them 'recovery runs' if these efforts are actually destroying their reactivity? In the Easy Interval method relaxed interval training is much preferred over a traditional recovery run.

Do a lot of aerobic training
Unfortunately, I have learnt that some runners get a little bit lazy when training according to the Easy Interval method and think that just running 12-15x200 and 8-10x400m would be enough to run a good 10km. These sessions may have a small benefit initially, but after a certain time the athlete will struggle to race much further than 5km. For races over 5km you do need to run a lot of aerobic mileage. The key, though, is that this shouldn't be just slow aerobic running, as I've discussed, but mostly intervals of 3-6 minutes and even a bit longer occasionally.

Extensive 400m intervals can also be considered an aerobic endurance run. The great Emil Zatopek was famous for doing sessions such as 60x400m. He would run one 400m at about his lactate-threshold velocity (72 seconds or even a bit slower), followed by an easy 200 or 400m. These are very long, more or less aerobic sessions but the key is that he was still running quickly for at least half of the run.

Implement periods without any anaerobic training
If you are a serious, competitive runner who occasionally implements anaerobic tempos, you should have building periods in which you skip any heavy anaerobic workouts altogether. Anaerobic training may force more anaerobic metabolism and less aerobic function, thus it can have a negative influence on aerobic muscle fibres and the aerobic muscle enzymes. During such periods the Easy Interval Method is a very good way of maintaining your running economy and reactivity without forcing yourself into a more anaerobic zone.

Some longer non-stop runs are necessary
Some shorter and longer endurance runs (always with surges) will benefit your aerobic power and stamina and are also essential in preparing for a marathon. I improved 40 seconds over 10,000m in just one winter after adding two morning 7-10km runs per week (some-times 6-8x1000m). The pace of these runs was moderate, but I would always make sure I had

a number of one-minute surges at a faster pace so I was never running in a continuous, slow fashion. These types of runs will benefit you for all distances. If training for shorter distances (1500-5000m), during a build-up period, you can perform these runs over 6-10km with a surge every 5-6 minutes. If training for races of 10-15km I would run 8-12km with a 30-60 second surge every five minutes. I would do these as a normal run around my favourite loops, but a variation - probably just as effective - could be a continuous run of 6x1000m with 1000m fast followed by 1000m easy.

An extra advantage of the Easy Interval Method

During my career I experienced another advantage of the Easy Interval Method as opposed to a more steady-state based approach. Suppose you are a middle-distance athlete training with steady-state running as basic training and midway through the racing season you begin to get tired or lose form. The traditional approach would be to rest for a few days and go back to your basic steady-state training to re-build your base until you have recovered and feel fit again. After 3-4 weeks you may start feeling fitter again, but you will have lost some reactivity, speed and running economy from the slower running and so will then need to do another few weeks of interval training to get back to where you were.

When training according to the Easy Interval Method you will get a much quicker return to form. You will take a few days off and then re-start your basic easy intervals, maybe going a bit slower than you were initially and doing fewer repetitions to begin with, until you start feeling fitter again. Because you will still be running quicker during the intervals, I can almost guarantee that after a month you will be in reasonable shape. You will have maintained your reactivity and running economy and at the same time your aerobic endurance will not decrease.

5.2 Anaerobic training

Many serious track runners often do two hard anaerobic sessions and a race every week. They feel this is necessary to run fast at distances from 800 to 5000m. However, as you have read in my schedule of 1974 in chapter 3, I made a huge breakthrough, for example going from 9:00 to 8:15 over 3000m, seemingly without any anaerobic training. How was that possible?

Limit the number of your anaerobic workouts

The explanation is actually very simple: my anaerobic endurance was built by running races (from 800-5000m) nearly every weekend, and this one anaerobic (race) effort worked perfectly for me. A race is a very specific anaerobic workout whereby at the end of each race you are running heavily in the anaerobic zone. These races are perfect for training the lactate capacity in muscles and also boosting VO2max. The rest of my week was all easy interval training which still trained VO2max, lactate threshold and enabled me to run at high speeds, while still recovering from the race. This initial experience convinced me that only one hard, anaerobic session or race every week was enough to perform very well. This is very true for many runners and there are few athletes who are able to consistently run twice-weekly hard, anaerobic sessions plus a race without breaking down.

What is specific training for middle-distance runners?

A very common misconception among track athletes (800-5000m) is that specific training is very hard anaerobic training. They believe that to get the best anaerobic endurance (the best usage, the best clearance of lactate), they have to do a lot of very hard, anaerobic training where they reach as high as possible lactic acid levels. This is often seen as very specific, quality interval training. However, my point of view is that this is not specific, because now they are working at a level of lactate that is much higher than they will achieve during the 'cruising' phase of a race. Why train a lot at a level that they will perhaps only reach during the last phase of the race? Put another way: why would a 5000m runner train at lactate levels that are only reached by an 800m runner? You shouldn't spend an awful lot of time and effort training at these intensities which are largely useless in a race, and often more damaging than beneficial.

For the vast majority of people, running at high speed with high levels of lactate can only be maintained for a very short period of time. This so-called anaerobic lactate capacity is obviously very important in the final lap of a race, especially for middle-distance runners (800m-5000m). On the other hand, it is also important for middle-distance runners to keep lactate levels as low as possible during most of the race. However, a lot of hard, anaerobic training may force a greater use of the anaerobic metabolism and less of the aerobic metabolism (lactic acid produced during anaerobic training may inhibit aerobic muscle enzymes). When running a 5000m race, most of the energy (over 90%) is applied from an aerobic metabolism, and so your specific training should really be focussed on keeping lactate levels low. In other words, you should focus on training the lactate-clearing system (see chapter 4) that will be used for most of the race as opposed to the last minute.

The Easy Interval Method achieves this by running at different speeds under and just around the lactate threshold. It is right around the area between producing lactic acid and breaking down the waste products (H+ ions) and allows the athlete to practice the relaxed, fluid running action and cruising speed that they will be using during the race. I would regularly run 40-70 quality km per week at a fast but comfortable pace in order to achieve this balance. This is in stark contrast to the 'traditional' approach of the elite and even average competitive runner who totals about 10km per week of very hard, anaerobic training which is not specific - as has been discussed in the paragraphs before - but overkill and potentially damaging to the athlete. For well-trained runners some anaerobic training is useful because it improves their VO2max and ability to buffer lactate and waste products, which is helpful in running fast at the end of a race despite being out of breath. However, for most of those runners, just one hard anaerobic effort a week in a pre-race build-up period should be sufficient. This can be done as a middle-distance race or a mixed session with alternating speeds and distances. I personally believe that mixed sessions (such as the one described in chapter 7.2) where the runner alternates between aerobic and anaerobic speeds provide a greater training stimulus. They are also easier to recover from. Only elite runners should consider adding an occasional extra anaerobic session in a pre-race build-up period.

This easy interval training (with just a little bit of anaerobic training) worked perfectly for me and so many other runners as mentioned in chapter 2. During my prime years I was tested for lactate levels and among other top national runners I was shown to be performing with the lowest levels of lactate. Interestingly, I was also able to run the fastest final lap in a race despite the fact that I had one of the slowest 100m times of all runners tested. The point being that despite other runners being faster than I was, they had used up more of their anaerobic energy during the first 90% of the race and so were unable to use it at the end. I had also achieved faster times over 1500m, 3000m and 5000m. Somewhat bizarrely though, instead of this being seen a wake-up call for the national coach that the other runners were not optimally trained, I was criticised for not training properly and was told to do more hard, anaerobic sessions so I could have a higher lactate level at the finish line!

Some years later a Swedish study, comparing the best Kenyans with the best Swedish distance runners, showed that the lower the lactate levels, the better the results of middle and long distance runners. The research showed that the Swedish runners had similar VO2max, running economy and muscle fibre type as the Kenyans (who easily beat them in races), but the study concluded that the Kenyans operated with much lower accumulation of lactate and the H+ ion waste products.

What is specific: race pace or race intensity? Don't overlook the adrenaline!

Given that I have discussed the importance of not training too fast in comparison to your race distance, you may be thinking that when training, say 1000m repeats, you may be better off doing them at race speed as opposed to lactate threshold. At first thought, it seems to make sense. There can't be anything else more specific than training at race speed, right? However, it's worth bearing in mind that during a workout there is a huge difference between race pace and race intensity. Let's take a simple example of a 15-minute 5km runner. Don't worry if you are slower than this level, the principles are the same whatever your pace. According to conventional training wisdom, a quality, specific training session for such a runner would be 4-6x1000m at race pace, or 3:00 per kilometre.

Unfortunately many coaches and runners overlook a few essential things.
- It's actually quite rare to run a race with perfectly even splits. A more regular occurrence is a faster start (getting carried away on adrenaline and excitement) followed by a few slow kilometres and then a strong finish. The end result is an average of 3:00 per kilometre without actually running a single one in three minutes.
- During most training sessions a runner is not at their peak, physically or mentally.

They may be tired from the previous day's training; their warm-up may not be as thorough as before a race and mentally they are not as focussed as they are in a race.

- A runner's best ever race will have probably been done under almost ideal conditions. The runner will have been well rested and tapered; they will have been wearing racing flats and will have focussed on the race for weeks beforehand. Other competitors will have pushed them along during the race itself. The adrenaline of the gun firing and the athlete entering 'race mode' is a huge factor and cannot be underestimated.

Given the above reasons I hold the opinion that for this runner a three-minute kilometre in a training session is too intense. The build-up of lactate will start too soon and reach very high levels whereas in a race we want to delay this process for as long as possible. I would advise this runner to start the session at around 3:20 per 1000m to make sure they are training the metabolism that will be used for 80-90% of the race. We are focussing on race intensity rather than race pace.

When I was running 5000m in around 13:45, doing tempos of 1000m at 2:45 (my actual 5000m race pace) felt more like 1500m effort than 5000m. Now you may wonder: "Don't I have to practice race pace?" Of course you do, but in the Easy Interval Method your muscles will get used to 5km race pace by running relaxed 200 and 400m intervals.

You may need more than a week to recover from a hard workout
Many athletes and coaches think that recovery after a heavy and comprehensive anaerobic workout takes place in just 2-3 days, because the excess lactate has disappeared within a day – actually within hours. However, after a hard, anaerobic workout your body can be stressed for much longer, due to leaking muscle cells, damaged enzymes and stress hormones. Once – after a very hard, anaerobic workout (an experiment) of 6x1000m – I experienced decreased performance more than a week later.

Dr Jan Olbrecht, a well-known Belgian physiologist, was quoted in Runner's World (July 2001, Dutch edition): "One of the remarkable aspects of anaerobic training is that if you train it too often, your anaerobic power will decrease." Olbrecht has pioneered the use of blood-lactate testing, particularly with swimmers, and his observations are based on practical experience with world and Olympic champions. It is striking that the godfather of the Easy Interval Method, Herman Verheul, came to the same conclusion in the 1970s and said that "If you do too much anaerobic training, your performance will decrease."

"I need to mention one of the physiological problems of scheduling hard anaerobic workouts for prolonged periods… eventually - especially if racing is added to hard interval training - there is a great risk that blood pH may not return to normal. When that happens, it can upset your ability to get nutrients out of food, upset the central nervous system, and manifest itself in a loss of performance and interest in running. In the end, excessive anaerobic training pulls down your VO2max and you can't even run the slow stuff very well." - Ron Daws, Running Your Best

I have seen many elite Dutch and European runners doing way too much anaerobic training. I came across a runner who ran a very respectable 3:41 for 1500m during the indoor season with only one anaerobic session a week. I met him again some months later at an outdoor meet in Italy where he ran over 3:50 for the same distance. He was very confused, as he said he had been doing three very hard anaerobic sessions every week and didn't know why he was racing slower.

Photo: Theo van de Rakt

The great Carlos Lopes, Olympic marathon champion in 1984 and multiple world cross-country champion, also made a point of avoiding heavy anaerobic work before big races. Three days before

Former 5000m world record holder Emiel Puttemans (51) and Klaas Lok (82) competing in a 15km road race in the Netherlands (April 1981). Puttemans won in 43:54, Lok finished second in 44:19.

the 1985 World Cross-country Championships the Portuguese squad met for an interval session of 15x400m with only 60-seconds rest. Lopes ran these in 64 seconds - which for a 13:17 5000m and 27:17 10,000m runner is very easy. The rest of the group charged round in 57-59 seconds, with Lopes coming in last on every repetition. Three days later Lopes became world champion, beating the best Kenyan and Ethiopian runners. The rest of the Portuguese team finished a long way down the field (I finished 49th, 1:15 behind Lopes). Another interesting note is that during that race Lopes ran the first kilometre in 2:47 and was 11 seconds off the leader. He maintained his pace through the whole 12km and won.

Why do so many runners do hard workouts so close to an important race? Maybe because they think their body needs to suffer even in the pre-race week in order to sharpen shape? That their body can recover within a few days? Or maybe because they are scared of losing shape when training is relaxed for that one week?

When you have done specific training for 6-8 weeks and a few races have shown that you are in shape, you should taper instead of taking risks by doing any hard training in the final week. Training hard in the last week won't help you anymore - relaxed training will! Any hard training in the week before a race will only make you tired.

During my career I learned the importance of tapering off before big events. One of my best races was a 3000m at the European indoor championships in 1978. I finished fifth in

7:51.4 and only two seconds behind world-class runners such as Markus Ryffel (5000m in 13:07, Olympic silver in 1984) and Emiel Puttemans (former 5000m world record holder). In chapter 3 you have already read my light schedule that week, with the final three days being extremely easy with just 2x400m easy in 1:14 the day before the race. This pace may seem fast to some runners, but please bear in mind that 7:51 for 3000m is an average pace of 62.8 seconds per 400m.

How to run your hard, long, anaerobic tempos?

As well as running too many hard, anaerobic sessions, a lot of runners perform these long interval tempos incorrectly, too. They will often start too fast for the first lap, within a minute their anaerobic system has more or less taken over and is too dominant. Remember again that in a 5000m your aerobic system contributes more than 90% of the energy. A runner should try to run in such a way that the second half of the effort is faster than the first half. This should be done by relaxing more in the first half to try and keep your aerobic system more dominant rather than forcing the pace too much near the end.

During my career we used to run the hard tempos in our mixed sessions in the forest by starting at a relaxed tempo and increasing the pace as we went. We used to have an 800m lap that we would do twice. Often the first 800m would be covered in 2:24 with the second one in 2:08. This was also often done with the last 400m in about 62 seconds and the last 200m in 28-30. Not only did this avoid me using my anaerobic system early on in the session, but it was also great practice for racing and learning how to finish fast at the end. I once finished the last 400m of a 5km race in 53.5 seconds - not bad for a runner with a meagre 12.5s 100m personal best.

By doing hard anaerobic tempos at a gradually increasing speed, you train yourself to delay the onset of excessive lactate levels. In this way you will probably be using the energy systems more or less in the same way as how you use them when racing. You might also learn how the speed feels at which these excessive lactate levels cause your legs to feel 'heavy'. This will teach you to prevent surpassing this critical speed too early. As a result you will be relatively fresh when you enter the final stage of a race in which you can 'open your anaerobic tank' and run a fast last one to two minutes. For me it is not a surprise that nearly all the runners I know who have trained using the Easy Interval Method as their basic training improved their finishing speed. In chapter 2.2 you have read some personal stories of runners who experienced this.

Criticism: 'You have to suffer!'

One of the most common criticisms of the Easy Interval method is that 'you do not learn to suffer the pain experienced in races due to the lack of hard, anaerobic training and so you will never be able to push yourself like other runners'. I do not agree with this assessment. I think it is more ingrained in the character of each athlete as to how much they can push themselves. Sport does not build character; it only helps to reveal it. As a 15-year-old I ran my first 5km training loop. I had never trained before and pushed myself hard the whole way, including sprinting at the end. I had never trained myself to tolerate pain, I just did it.

Furthermore, as discussed previously, too many hard and painful sessions increase the risk of fatigue and injury. In a race it is much better to feel like a caged lion waiting to be released! My experience has always been that when I was fit and ready, I could always give it my all and push my body to extraordinary lengths. If you're tired and worn out, no matter how much you 'want it', you can never push as hard as if you were fresh and ready.

Finally, when a runner is suffering and straining during training, it is impossible to develop a relaxed and fluid running style. You will be teaching yourself to run with tension and tightness as opposed to freely and easily. During the race your running should feel as relaxed and fluid as possible. If you spend too much time training in a strained and tight manner, you will do so in a race.

With my clubmate Joost Borm I ran 3:38 for 1500m and we did about a quarter of the hard, anaerobic training that most of the other top 1500m runners were doing. It was interesting that during a relay race over 3000m, where Joost and I had to run 15x200m all out, we beat the other teams of top Dutch athletes who were known for their many hard 200m sessions. A possible clue that a lot of easy interval training plus a little hard, anaerobic training makes you cope better with anaerobic waste products than steady-state training combined with a lot of hard, anaerobic training.

Unfortunately, many athletes and coaches still cannot accept that reduced anaerobic training can lead to better performance. They embrace the point of view "train hard, win easy". Running life would be simple if it were true that the more you put in, the more will come out. But - lucky for you! - it's not that simple. Based on so many experiences we now know that the Easy Interval Method is an excellent approach. So a better motto might be: 'train smart, win easy'!

Arthur Lydiard: "Anaerobic training is something we have to do if we intend to race well, but at the same time we must always keep in mind that if we overdo it we lose our most essential asset, the very thing we have been building, our good [aerobic] condition, which determines our performance level."

5.3   Strength training and the importance of reactivity

In general I am not a big fan of resistance (weight) training for distance runners, although I would make an exception for elite 800m runners, as you will read in chapter 11. Also, runners who are clearly lacking leg strength may benefit from some weight training. However, caution is advised. Strength training with weights can involve some risk with respect to the neuromuscular programming of your muscles, the fine tuning of every muscle fibre. Also, the specific elongation and pre-tension of your muscles built up in the landing phase during running does not take place while doing weight training. Strength training should mostly be specific, as similar to the running movement as possible.

Absolute strength is not really important for a runner; reactivity is. Reactive-strength/weight ratio is what really matters. Most of the elite East-African runners are actually far weaker than their Western counterparts. They have very thin legs, but it is all reactivity and 'bounce' that you see when you watch them run. Having or not having good reactivity can make quite a difference in performance, as you have learned in chapter 5.1 from Finnish researcher Laina Paavolainen. My advice is to include some reactivity training in every workout, preferably at the end of your warm-up. The minimum you should do is some hops and bounding plus 3-4 relaxed sprints increasing in speed. I also advise well-trained runners to do a few sessions dedicated to just flat but relaxed 100m runs. Even a long distance runner can benefit greatly from increase in reactivity and strength.

Apart from running 100's, here are a few suggestions of other exercises to train your reactivity:
- Jumping rope.
- Hopping on one foot (be careful, this can be quite taxing; start on a soft surface if you can).
- On two feet, perform two small bounces followed by a high jump.
- Hop uphill with feet together.
- Jump from one foot to the other.
- Jumping like in the first figure below.
- Squat jumps. There's no need to go deeper than a 90 degree angle in your knees (see second figure). Try to perform these jumps on your forefoot, in a very quick, explosive manner, without stretching your body completely when moving upwards. When you don't fully stretch out, you can perform them with a higher frequency.

Jumping with two feet; try to bring your feet together in mid-air

Squat jumps on forefoot

5.4 Advice for young runners

I strongly oppose slow, monotonous endurance training for young runners, as you will already appreciate. Too much slow endurance training might turn a youngster into a 10km (or even longer distance) runner, while it is possible that their real talent is at 1500m. Although it is reversible, it is not desirable to take the risk of missing out on a talented middle-distance runner.

That being said, I would be in favour of a young runner doing a few 5-10km road races every year. They must have sufficient training and ability to run this distance but a few such races can provide a good stimulus for a young athlete's endurance. However, I would also be very wary of a youngster running too many 800-1500m races due to the anaerobic aspect of not only the races but the training that often goes with them. A young runner needs to focus on building their aerobic base with easy intervals as opposed to very hard, anaerobic sessions.

Intense anaerobic sessions are very taxing and stressful for even an experienced runner, but for a younger or novice runner

Photo: Theo van de Rakt

International meeting in 1978 featuring Holland, Portugal, Belgium, Austria, Denmark, Ireland, Wales and Luxembourg. Belgium runner Rik Schoofs leads in the 5000m, but Klaas Lok (left) wins with a fast last 400m in 53.5 seconds.

they are even worse. The anaerobic system should preferably and mainly be lightly stimulated with easy intervals over 200 or 400m. Together with a few races I feel that this is more than enough anaerobic training for the first years of their running career. Too much stress at this point in their development will potentially have a detrimental effect on their aerobic ability both now and in their future. For elite young runners competing in national and international championships I would strongly limit any anaerobic sessions to only once a week and only for about 5-6 weeks at a time in a final preparation period.

From the outset it will be clear that training for a young distance runner should be all-round and mainly consist of a mix of easy intervals of 100 to 1000m, small numbers of reps, which in the beginning gradually increase. In addition, they will benefit from some speed and hill training, a limited number of moderately fast endurance runs with surges and running races over a variety of distances. Physiologist Jan Olbrecht: *"At a young age you should try to improve as much as possible with as little training as possible"*.

6. Easy interval basic training pace guidelines & table

This chapter will look at the suggested paces at which you should be running your basic easy interval training. Firstly, I will give you guidelines for the interval training based on race paces (except for 100m's). Secondly, I will include a pace table, which I have placed at the end of this chapter. I have also included guidelines for the scarce non-stop endurance runs (with surges). All the paces are determined by your *current* race fitness and not goal fitness or past performances. If your personal best is from two years ago but you are not in the same shape currently, please be honest with yourself or you will run the risk of training too fast. In the table I only use a current 10km performance as a starting point, but further on in this chapter you will find that track runners can also use their 1500-3000m race paces.

I should also point out that I have taken into account that on an average training day you will not be at your peak race fitness. Your personal best time was most likely set on fresh, tapered legs in a competitive environment with the adrenaline flowing. It is impossible to replicate these conditions by yourself and so I have amended the suggested paces accordingly.

The suggested paces are presumed to be run in good training conditions and on a firm surface. If, for example, you are running 1000m's on grass and wearing a tracksuit, you should run at least a handful seconds slower compared to a session on a tartan track in shorts and a singlet. For runners who have never performed any interval training before I would suggest they start even slower than advised here, reduce the number of repetitions and build up over a period of months. Do not be a slave to the paces, either. If you are tired or the weather is bad then don't force yourself to hit the paces. Accept that today is a bad day and adjust accordingly.

If you have a heart-rate monitor: I have included guideline heart rates that are applicable for aerobic sessions over 1000-2000m and endurance runs. Another device to monitor your intensity is the Stryd running power meter, which has the advantage that it immediately registers your intensity (so it can also be used at shorter intervals). Please find all the information on the internet. Runners who like to keep things simple can gloss over the heart rate information and just use the guidelines, table and their easy interval running feel.

All intervals are performed with a flying start.

The table at the end of the chapter does not include any paces for your anaerobic sessions - these are a different story!

Easy 100m intervals

The paces for the 100m repetitions are not set in stone and are very much dependent on feel. They should be used to add some spring and bounce back into your legs (see chapter 5.1) as opposed to being very hard and damaging. If you are fresh (maybe before the session) I suggest you try and run these 100m repetitions slightly faster than your 200m intervals which, for most runners, is about 800-1500m race pace. If you are tired (maybe after a session of 6x1000m) then I suggest you run these 100m repetitions on feel. You could finish your main session, do some gentle stretching and have a few minutes recovery. The first 100m could then be done slightly faster than the pace of your main session. Each repetition can be performed slightly faster if you feel good and the final one may be quicker than your usual 200m pace.

After a long endurance run of 1-2 hours you should be extra careful. Your muscles may be tired and stiff and so do not jump straight into a very fast 100m - always gradually increase the speed to reduce any injury risk.

The rest for the 100m's is 100m walk/jog back to the start. If performing the 100m's as a separate session, advanced runners could do a set of 15-25x100m, or even alternate non-stop 100m fast with 100m easy and so on for the prescribed number of repetitions. Former Belgian 5000m world record holder Emiel Puttemans told me one of his sessions was to alternate 50m very fast (6-7 seconds) with 50m moderate (9-10 seconds) for 3000m. He managed to run the entire 3000m in 8:00 this way (his PB was 7:37). Not for the faint-hearted!

Easy 200m intervals

The pace of the 200m intervals corresponds to roughly 1500-3000m race pace. The recovery is 200m, which is composed of a jog or easy run, and a short walk of 10-20 seconds at start and end of the rest. It might be tempting to start these short 200m's too fast, but control yourself and run the complete session in a fast but relaxed pace, although starting the first 1-2 reps a tiny bit slower could be wise. If you have never run a 1500 or 3000m race, you could use a race predictor calculator from the internet, using your 10km time as a starting point. However, be aware that the outcome will be your potential race times. If you are a long-distance runner, having done mainly steady-state training, you will probably be stuck in a 'long distance pace' and - assuming your goal would be to run those times - will need a year or so before being able to perform the calculated times. This means that you will need to add a few seconds per 200m (as well as for your 400m intervals) compared to your calculated 1500-3000m race paces and also to the prescribed times in the table.

Easy 400m intervals

These are being run at a pace that corresponds to approximately 10km race pace. For very slow runners this could even be 5km pace and for elite runners maybe 10-20km pace.

Recovery is 400m which is composed of a jog or easy run, and a short walk of 10-20 seconds at start and end of the rest.

Note - Due to the 200-400m intervals being so short I do not advise you monitor your lactate threshold (LT) heart rate. It takes the heart rate 1-1.5 minutes or more to stabilise with an accurate reading and as the running velocities are above the LT-velocity, it does not make sense to try and run according to your heart rate. You can, of course, use your heart-rate monitor but do not be a slave to it and do not try to run the short distances at below your LT-velocity. I've heard of runners who desperately reported that they did not succeed to stay under their LT-velocity at the 200 and 400m tempos.

Easy 1000m intervals

For most runners these are run around zone 3 which will generally correlate to a pace that is between their 10km and half-marathon race pace. For elite runners these are often run outside half-marathon and closer to their marathon pace. Many times I would do 8x1000m at around my marathon pace or even slower - remember that such a 1000m session is an aerobic session. For runners with a 10km of around one hour things are a little bit different. Remember that lactate threshold (LT) pace can only be maintained for approximately 45-60 minutes. So, a runner whose 10km time is around 60-62 minutes may have an LT pace that is faster than their 10km pace. This is why these runners should run the 1000m intervals closer to their 10km speed compared to faster runners. Runners of 65 minutes and slower will possibly train faster than their 10km race speed. As mentioned earlier, they could also consider changing 1000m's into 800m's.

Please be aware that some LT pace calculators on the internet will calculate your LT pace based on your personal best race pace performed under perfect conditions and filled with adrenaline. Unfortunately, those websites will then advise you paces for your longer aerobic interval training based on *this* LT pace, without adjusting for your slower LT pace under training conditions, which could be a hand full of seconds slower per 1000m.

For example, I ran my best 10km at 2:50.4/km (this means a cruising speed of about 2:51.5; the race was under ideal circumstances, I was filled with adrenaline, I ran in spikes and on a tartan track) which - on that day, in that race - gave a LT pace of approximately 2:55-2:58 min/km. However, I estimate that on normal training days in that same period my LT was probably around 3:00-3:03 and for sure slower in other periods. That's why I rarely ran my 1000m easy intervals faster than 3:10 and when training in the forest in flats I mostly ran 3:12-3:20. At the start of a building period, for a couple of weeks, I went as slow as 3:25. This may still sound very fast for many readers but remember I was able to run a 10km race at 2:50.4 per km.

In the table I have taken this difference into account, to help you avoid running your longer aerobic, easy intervals too fast.

Instead of using your 10km pace (as the table suggests) you can choose to do a time trial of 30 minutes (as described in chapter 4) to determine your LT pace and then run your 1000m intervals slightly slower.

For those who are experienced with training to their heart rate (please note that the percentages are not 100% accurate for all), the 1000m intervals should generally be run at approximately 92-95% of their LT heart rate. During a final pre-race building period you can occasionally run a bit faster but limit such sessions to just once or twice a week for about four weeks in total. At the start of a build-up and during a busy race period you should go even slower than the 92-95%. The times in the table are based on good conditions. Don't forget: calculate your LT heart rate during training conditions (see chapter 4). Also keep in mind that performing many sessions, for many weeks, too close to your LT pace will be too stressful. Always listen to your body: when you are not fit, or if you are tired from previous training, please moderate your speed. For example, if training for a marathon it is normal that you won't be in top shape as you will be tired from additional long runs. In these instances it is safer to apply the lowest heart rate or use the slowest times in the table. Generally, it is far better to be ten seconds too slow than one second too fast!

The rest between the 1000m intervals is 800m (or even 1000m), which is composed of a jog or easy run, and a short walk of 10-20 seconds at start and end of the rest.

Easy 2000m intervals (or miles if you prefer a shorter interval)

These are to be run at a slightly lower intensity than your 1000m intervals, which will generally correlate to high in zone 2 and occasionally the lower end of zone 3. I must emphasise a degree of caution when implementing the 2000m's into your schedule. I would recommend only well-trained runners implement these and when performing 2000m intervals, you should be disciplined. If you start a bit too fast, the first half may still feel easy but you are at risk that during the last 2-3 minutes your effort will get too intense. However, this is supposed to be an aerobic workout in which you should feel strong and relaxed for the entire duration of the 2000m. The heart rate during the interval will generally be around 90% of your LT heart rate. The rest between reps is 1000m easy running/jogging and a short walk of 10-20 seconds at start and end of the rest.

Fast endurance run of around 6-10km with surges

The basic pace of these runs in the Easy Interval Method is comfortably fast - about the same pace as your slowest 1000m easy intervals (so roughly the same heart rate is applicable). Every 5-7 minutes there is a surge which can be anything from 30-60 seconds or a bit longer and will be run at around your tempo pace (see chapter 4). You can, of course, vary the pace and duration of the surge, so your 30-second surge may be faster than your one-minute surge.

Moderate endurance run of around 8-12 km with surges

This is a relaxed, moderately paced run, and for those with a heart-rate monitor: your basic pace should be at an intensity in the lower range of zone 2, which correlates to approximately 85% of your LT heart rate. Every 5-7 minutes there is a surge for 30-60 seconds up to your easiest 1000m interval pace.

Easy, long endurance run of around 25-30 km with surges

These are easy runs and can go as long as 35km if training for a marathon. The heart rate of the basic speed should be about 75-80% of your LT heart rate. A surge of 30 seconds every 8-10 minutes is advised, which can go as fast as marathon pace. These runs can be up to two hours or more, so the surge shouldn't be too fast or too long as it may be too tiring. You could think of these runs as a slightly more structured fartlek or a very relaxed 200m interval session, but with longer recoveries. The difference being the recovery: not jogging but a constant easy endurance pace.

Endurance run of around 15-20 km with surges

These runs can fit in between the moderate and long runs and can be used if training for a half or full marathon. The pace can vary between easy and moderate with surges of 30-60 seconds every 6-8 minutes, which can go as fast as half-marathon pace.

Mixed training in the forest

This session consists of sprints, hill runs, short and long intervals as well as exercises (core stability and bounding, etc). In your build-up or base phase the longer intervals will be mainly aerobic (LT speed or slower). During a pre-race period some anaerobic intervals will be implemented but these are preferably done on 'feel' (and at increasing speed, as explained in chapter 5.2) as opposed to strictly controlled by a watch. You can also do your anaerobic sessions on a track or measured course and I give examples of these in chapter 7.3. An example of a mixed session can be found in chapter 7.2.

Heart-rate percentages don't fit everybody

As already mentioned: be aware that the heart-rate percentages are just a guide and will not be applicable for all. Slower runners especially should take note as they often have an LT pace that covers a larger span while in faster runners the LT can be more accurately pinpointed.

Also note that a faster runner might have an easy running pace of 14km/h and a LT of 19km/h, which means their aerobic area of comfortable running is 5km/h. A slower runner, however, may have an easy running pace of 9km/h and an LT of 11km/h which means a slight acceleration can take them from easy to out of breath and above the lactate threshold.

A word of caution: I have heard of quite a few runners who had incorrectly determined their LT or maximum heart rate, leading to training at incorrect intensities, so please make sure you test accurately.

Finally, the weather can have a dramatic impact on your heart rate. In very warm conditions your heart rate will be higher than normal and your LT speed and LT heart rate can be different on a daily basis. I would advise you spend a few weeks or months getting used to training with a heart-rate monitor so you are confident in its accuracy and how your body feels in certain training zones.

Train on feel, guided by race pace intensity, or use the table?

The previous paragraphs explaining the target paces are very much guidelines. Generally, the basic interval training should be guided by your feeling of the pace as discussed in this chapter. Also, the paces in the table should be seen as a guide. I would use the table as a starting point if you have a recent 10km time and go from there. Some runners also choose to be guided by a heart-rate monitor. When you start to feel more familiar with your LT, you can determine the pace of your longer aerobic intervals. Remember that we are not machines; always keep in mind that you should run your basic interval training 'fast but relaxed, with a comfortable feeling', as my coach Verheul used to say.

Dutchman Jos Verdaasdonk said: "Even with headwind I tried to run my 2000m intervals in the scheduled time; I felt I didn't train right when I ran slower. Then I started using a heart monitor and realised I was running too intensely. Now I run more controlled and don't care about the exact times. As long as my intensity is right, I feel I am training in a correct manner."

The table doesn't fit everybody

The training times I have suggested in the table are estimations and do generally fit well for 5-10km runners who are used to interval training. Older runners and runners who are mainly used to slower, steady-state training may find the paces of the 200-400m intervals too fast and so – as already mentioned in the paragraph about 200m's – they should add a few seconds onto each repetition until they are more relaxed at this speed. Changes in training will mean your body will have to adapt to the new stimulus, so when starting out always go slower than you perhaps think you should. Runners who have done no intervals or faster training would also be advised to do some hill training and bounding as their reactivity is probably very poor.

You should use a recent 10km race where you performed very well while fresh and tapered. It should be on a fast course in good conditions. When you are tired or sore after a race, please use some common sense - slow down your training paces or cut the number of repetitions and do not blindly use your race pace or table as reference. Learn to 'feel' your comfortable easy interval pace. In the days coming up to a peak race I would recommend you cut the number of repetitions down and also reduce the pace. I would often do my 400m's in just 76 seconds and 200m's in 35-36 compared to 72-70 and 33-31 that I would normally do.

Start with the slow times and if necessary stay there

At the beginning of an aerobic build-up phase you should always use the times at the slower end of the range. Month after month you can slowly run a bit faster - ideally this will just happen naturally without you pushing any harder. But if you need to push yourself then keep applying the slow times; remember that the long intervals are aerobic sessions! In chapter 7 I will discuss the harder, anaerobic sessions that some runners need.

Do you walk shortly after and before an interval?

Historically in the Easy Interval Method, after doing an easy interval tempo, we'd gradually come to a standstill and continue with a short walk of 10-20 seconds (time is on feel). We'd then jog or run at an easy pace for most of the recovery distance, before walking the last 10-20 seconds in preparation for the next faster tempo. This has been mentioned in the paragraphs earlier on. I should make the point that this isn't set in stone and some well-trained runners occasionally prefer not to do the short walking breaks to stress their aerobic system a bit more. Occasionally, non-stop interval training will also be useful during a marathon preparation.

You might argue that when you want to perform a longer distance race non-stop – such as a 10km - you also need to run non-stop for such distances in training several times a week. This is not true. Most people can build up quite easily to running a certain distance without stopping. The real challenge is running that distance faster than before.

As you would have guessed there isn't any scientific research, but experience has shown that even well-trained runners fare better when they implement the walking breaks. Personally, I nearly always had a short walking break when I was training and, just like many others, I found it helped my muscles relax and I felt it made it easier to control the pace of the quicker tempos through the session. I also found it helped me to recover more easily and so reduced my risk of injury or getting overtrained.

However, sometimes I would skip the walking on my morning run of e.g. 8x1000m and slow the pace down slightly for my quicker efforts. When I was training for a marathon or half marathon, I occasionally did a 'Zatopek-session'. This consisted of running continuously for an hour and alternating 400m at half marathon pace with 400m at an easy pace.

In general, my advice is to mostly implement the walking breaks. Only when you are well-trained and aiming for distances of 10km and longer, should you consider doing one non-stop interval session a week (preferably not the 200's). This is alongside your race or an endurance run with surges at the weekend. However, when you have one or two extra mid-week endurance runs with surges (which are present in some schedules for very well-trained runners) I advise you to do the walking breaks in all the interval sessions. Please be aware that skipping the walking breaks could cause less relaxed running and more effort to complete your session. Unfortunately making every session a bit too heavy for many weeks is less effective and could even lead to overtraining. I suggest running your tempos slightly slower if you prefer to skip the walking breaks. Obviously, by implementing the walking breaks you can more easily run the scheduled times and may find you feel better. You may also be training with others and the walking breaks provide a nice time for a chat between repetitions.

As I mentioned before, I can't actually prove which way is better, but in my experience I am sure that the walking breaks provide extra relaxation for the muscles and so they will - apart from the benefits mentioned earlier - develop better running economy. I am a strong believer that middle-distance athletes (800-5000m) should nearly always implement the short walks, especially during their track season when they need to be fresh for races. For runners focusing on 10km and longer races I would advise on always doing the walking breaks in the two days before a race and during the final week before a peak race. In general my personal preference is to mostly use the walking breaks (as masters world-record holders John van der Wansem and Silke Schmidt also do), but occasionally well-trained runners can skip these in order to stress their aerobic system a bit more.

The length of the recovery jog is also not set in stone. Some athletes prefer to do these sessions in a more natural environment and so, instead of 400m fast & 400m slow, they will set their watch to beep every 90 seconds and run fast for 90 seconds with 90 seconds slow. Please note that equal time is not the same as equal distance when it comes to recovery. When training by distance the actual time of the recovery is a lot longer than the effort of the faster run. When doing 400m in 90 seconds, a 400m jog will take closer to three minutes. If you decide to use time for your intervals please adjust your paces accordingly by running the quicker efforts slower than you normally would. The pace of the recovery jog is dependent on the athlete as well. Some will simply jog, while others often feel okay after about 20-30 seconds and will naturally increase their speed to an easy endurance pace, especially on the longer intervals.

Why is the recovery so long?
The recovery running between the intervals in the basic training is quite long - e.g. when doing an easy 1000m session the recovery is 800m (some runners even use 1000m). Critics will say this is far too long and that 1000m repeats can easily be done with 1-2 minutes recovery. The recoveries in the Easy Interval Method, however, are an important part of the session and so a 1000m interval workout can be considered similar to an easy aerobic run with surges of 1000m. Doing a full 800-1000m recovery jog provides a far greater aerobic stimulus than just jogging 200m, simply due to the extra mileage being covered. Remember that these easy intervals are your basic training and so you need to compare these sessions with what most consider basic training - the steady run. Let's say runner A runs steady for one hour at 15km/h. Runner B performs an easy interval session of 6x1000m with the 1000m efforts at 18km/h and the 800-1000m recovery jogs at 12km/h. Both sessions take roughly the same time and cover a similar distance (assuming runner B does a brief warm-up

and cool-down jog). In my view runner B has performed a vastly more effective workout. Both are aerobic sessions, but runner B has accumulated 6km worth of running at a quick, aerobic pace and broken up the monotonous slow training with its many disadvantages.

What if you are short on time?

I have often been asked the following question: "When short on time, is it better to do 4x1000m at the scheduled pace with full (800-1000m) recovery or 6x1000m a bit slower with shorter recovery (400m)?" Firstly, I would suggest you skip any non-essential parts of your warm-up and cool-down on days when you are on a tight schedule, as that may give you an extra few minutes to fit your session in. If you are still short on time, I would suggest doing all the reps (6x1000m with 400m recovery) but slower.

Finally, on the next page, you will find the table with estimated training times which can be used as a starting point for your easy interval paces. I would like to re-emphasise that these paces are guidelines and some runners may be slightly outside these ranges. If the conditions for training are bad, adjust your times accordingly. I can't emphasise often enough the importance of performing the basic interval training in a relaxed manner. For those who prefer to run miles as opposed to 2000m I would still urge you to run at the same pace as suggested for the 2000m intervals.

Coaches Lex van Eck van der Sluijs and Herman Verheul in 1984.

Photo: archive Lex van Eck van der Sluijs

recent 10km mins	2000m easy interval min:sec	1000m easy interval min:sec	400m easy interval min:sec	200m easy interval sec
28	6:44-6:24	3:15-3:02	1:14-1:07	34-30
29	6:56-6:36	3:21-3:08	1:14-1:08	34-31
30	7:08-6:48	3:27-3:14	1:15-1:09	34-31
31	7:20-7:00	3:34-3:20	1:17-1:11	35-32
32	7:34-7:14	3:40-3:26	1:19-1:13	36-33
33	7:48-7:28	3:46-3:32	1:22-1:16	37-34
34	8:02-7:40	3:53-3:39	1:24-1:18	38-34
35	8:16-7:54	4:00-3:45	1:26-1:20	39-35
36	8:30-8:06	4:06-3:51	1:29-1:23	40-36
37	8:42-8:20	4:13-3:57	1:31-1:25	41-37
38	8:54-8:30	4:18-4:02	1:33-1:27	42-38
39	9:08-8:42	4:25-4:08	1:36-1:30	44-39
40	9:20-8:54	4:31-4:14	1:39-1:32	45-40
41	9:32-9:08	4:37-4:20	1:41-1:34	46-41
42	9:46-9:20	4:44-4:26	1:43-1:36	47-42
43	10:00-9:32	4:50-4:32	1:45-1:38	48-43
44	10:14-9:46	4:57-4:38	1:47-1:40	49-44
45	10:26-9:58	5:03-4:44	1:49-1:42	50-45
46	10:38-10:10	5:09-4:50	1:51-1:44	51-46
47	10:52-10:22	5:15-4:56	1:53-1:46	52-47
48	11:04-10:34	5:21-5:01	1:55-1:48	53-48
49	11:16-10:46	5:27-5:07	1:57-1:50	55-50
50	11:28-10:58	5:33-5:12	1:59-1:52	56-51
51	11:40-11:10	5:38-5:17	2:01-1:53	57-52
52	11:52-11:20	5:44-5:23	2:03-1:55	58-53
53	12:04-11:32	5:50-5:29	2:05-1:57	59-54
54	12:16-11:44	5:56:5:34	2:07-1:59	60-55
55	12:28-11:56	6:01-5:39	2:09-2:01	61-56
56	12:38-12:06	6:07-5:44	2:11-2:03	62-57
57	12:50-12:16	6:12-5:49	2:13-2:05	63-58
58	13:02-12:28	6:18-5:55	2:15-2:07	65-59
59	13:12-12:38	6:23-6:00	2:17-2:09	66-61
60	13:24-12:50	6:29-6:05	2:19-2:11	67-62

If you want to convert the times into speed in km/h, use the calculation of these examples:
1km in 3:35 min:sec equals 1km in 215 seconds, then speed = 1/215*3600 = 16.74 km/h.
400m in 1:38 equals 400m in 98 secs, then speed = 0.4/98*3600=14.7 km/h.
200m in 45 secs, then speed = 0.2/45*3600 =16.0 km/h.

7. How to use the schedules - Mixed & anaerobic workouts

7.1 How to use the schedules

The following chapter provides advice and guidance on how to best apply the schedules to your own training.

For runners who have come from a mainly steady-state training background, I urge you to read the paragraph 'Changing from steady-state to easy interval training' below. For many runners, using the Easy Interval Method will be very different to what they have done before. The schedules often use the standard number of repetitions - 15x200, 10x400 and 6x1000m - which are aimed at runners who are used to frequent interval training. For those less experienced with regular interval training I would encourage you to reduce the number of intervals to start with and also run at a slower pace than prescribed. Always listen to your body and have patience: it may take you many months or even a year to get used to this new way of training.

The schedules are very much guidelines and principles that I hope the runner can use and apply to his or her own training. You can always adjust certain sessions to suit what you think may benefit you the most. For example, a runner may get great benefit from the shorter 200m sessions if they have never worked on training faster before and so may feel they prefer to do two of these sessions a week. Another runner may feel that their aerobic ability is not fully enhanced and so choose to focus on two or even three 1000m sessions.

Changing from steady-state to easy interval training

If you have never (or rarely) done any form of interval training before then here are some ideas:

- Start by implementing just one easy interval session a week for the first month or two. For example, on week 1 you can do some 1000m intervals, week 2 can be 400m's, etc. I would also suggest running the intervals slower and start with fewer repetitions. Gradually increase the number of repetitions and after a couple of months, or when you feel ready, you can try two interval sessions a week. After a few months you should be able to build up to the basic training of 12-15x200m, 8-10x400 and 4-6x1000m with a race or endurance run at the weekend.
- You change your entire training schedule overnight, but then you should train much slower than the paces given in chapter 6. You should also limit the number of intervals, e.g. start with 6x400m instead of 10x.

For older runners (60+) I would urge even more caution. The older we get, the slower our bodies recover and so a change in training will have an increased risk of injury. However, it is worth trying, because I do know of older runners that have reported progress in their race times within six months of changing to the Easy Interval Method.

'The schedules in this book look similar for whatever distance'

I am often challenged on the fact that most of the schedules that are prescribed are very similar regardless of the race distance that the runner is training for. Bizarrely, this comment is mainly from coaches who advocate steady-state training all year round, even for 800-1500m runners! My response is that from distances of 1500m to the marathon, the energy supplied from the aerobic system is 70-100%. It is therefore completely logical that a large part of the training for these distances should consist of aerobic sessions such as easy 1000m intervals. Also, the aerobic system is very trainable and can be improved considerably. Secondly, reactivity and running economy is important for a middle distance runner as well as a marathon runner - running fast is running fast regardless of distance - and so interval training over 200 and 400m is required. This is why a 1500m runner and a marathon runner can effectively do several sessions together - assuming a similar level of fitness - as their basic training is very similar.

When to make your schedule heavier (e.g. 8x1000m, 4-5x2000m)

Your aerobic training is very important in your overall development as a runner, so you will need to consider trying to do more of these sessions if you can. However, each athlete is different in terms of how much extra mileage they can run, stay healthy and benefit from. For a well-trained 10km runner this usually occurs around 60-70 miles per week. If your progression stagnates after a couple of years training according to the Easy Interval Method, then consider increasing your mileage. You could add an extra aerobic session of 6x1000m to your weekly schedule or you could increase your current session to 8x1000m. You could also add an extra 8-12km endurance run with surges (maybe as a morning run when training twice a day) or 4-5x2000m. These heavier weeks could be offset by a lighter week with reduced mileage every now and then. Finally, you could also consider a purely aerobic build-up period - as described in the 10km schedules in chapter 8 - where you focus more on the longer aerobic sessions.

Runners who are slower than 45 minutes for 10km should realise that doing the 2000m sessions is quite time consuming. Consider adding another session of 1000m intervals instead or, if you do want to go longer, running one mile intervals would be an option, or you could limit your number of 2000m's to just three.

When to make your schedule lighter (e.g. 12x200m, 8x400)

If you find the standard schedules in chapters 8 and beyond a little too heavy or difficult, I would advise you to run fewer repetitions than stated there. For example, 10-12x200m, 6-8x400m and 4-5x1000m. Another variation would be to alternate a harder week with an easier week - one week you could do the full number of repetitions and the next you could cut the sessions a bit shorter. Lastly, you could perform all the scheduled sessions one week, the next week cut one out completely and have a rest day.

More aerobic training and no progress: check your running economy

It's worth keeping in mind that adding more and more mileage may not actually have a positive effect. If you are adding more mileage and not improving, then I would urge you to look more at your reactivity and running economy. Adding in a few 100m runs before or after your main session as well as hopping and bounding exercises, may be far more beneficial for you than adding more miles.

Interval training without walking breaks

Sometimes in the schedules you will find a session like 6x1000m without walking. These are non-stop workouts in which during the recovery you skip the walking break. I would only advise these for reasonably well-trained runners who should benefit from the extra aerobic stimulus. It is also useful for marathon runners and can be used to replace endurance runs with surges. I would also advise you run these sessions a little slower than normal as the recovery might be reduced.

Tiredness and fatigue - Listen to your body

Runners who train regularly sometimes need a lighter day to help recovery. Competitive runners with an experienced coach, training six times (or more) a week, usually alternate three heavy days with one easy day and often have one day off (which may include cross training). They also have a lighter week every now and then where the volume and intensity are greatly reduced. When you are training regularly, feeling tired or having a bad day can happen and is nothing to worry about. But if you have prolonged periods of tiredness (over a week) where your legs feel heavy and sluggish, please be sensible and back off. If you do not scale back your training or have a day off, you risk overtraining which can take weeks or month to recover from.

Active rest periods

If you have a long racing period (3-4 months) you need a recovery period of 4-6 weeks without any races along with reducing both the volume and intensity of your sessions. I was guilty of not doing this myself and I have observed others repeat my error. When training and races are going very well, we often get carried away and keep racing and racing. Suddenly your form may deteriorate and you will begin struggling with races and your motivation to train will drop. It is wise to stay in control and plan ahead with a down period after a heavy racing schedule.

If you usually run almost every day, I would advise not only not racing in your rest period of 4-6 weeks, but also scaling down your training for at least three weeks. I would still advocate running, because when you build up again after a period of complete inactivity, you have a higher risk of stiff muscles and injury, which is why I call for active rest periods. In such a period the intensity and volume is reduced significantly compared to normal.

For an athlete normally running 5-7 times a week this could mean only running three times in the first week, followed by 3-4 times in the next 2-3 weeks. These sessions could also be lighter (e.g. 10x200, 6x400 and 4x1000m. Athletes who normally run four times a week, can cut out just one of their usual sessions and reduce the pace and volume of their other workouts. Runners with three running days don't need to cut out any workouts, just skipping a few tempos will be sufficient. This reduction in training, along with no racing, will help recover and rejuvenate the body after a hard racing period. Runners who only train one or two times a week don't need to reduce their training; just skipping races for one month should be enough.

Another tip would be to use this recovery period to focus on your reactivity by perhaps running more of your 200m intervals and even adding in a special session of 15-20x100m.

Better to train 7 times in 6 days than 7 times in 7 days

This rule is applicable when you are a serious, competitive runner who wants to train every day. It means that I advise you to take one day off a week and have a double day, instead of training every day without any rest. The day off will reduce your chance of getting tired and also helps to reduce your risk of injury. On your 'double day' make sure you do two different sessions that have focus on different intensities. For example, I would suggest 6-8x1000m in the morning and then 15x200m in the afternoon, as opposed to doing two sessions of 1000m intervals.

Two-day rule

Be aware of the 'two-day rule': after a heavy session or race it will generally take you two days before you are reasonably fit and feeling good again. That is why I would advise you to take two light days before and after a (heavy) race. Many people often have the second day before a race as their rest day and then a light training session the day before. For example, if you are racing Sunday, take Friday off and then train lightly on Saturday. Obviously, you will not be fully recovered from a hard race after just two days but you should be over the worst and can start thinking of training normally again. This doesn't apply to a marathon - and for many runners a half marathon - where it can take a lot longer to fully recover.

Train more relaxed in race season

Another aspect to monitor closely is the intensity of your interval training during a racing period. If you are racing every week - without peaking for a key race - then you need to do your basic training slower than you normally would. You need to be especially careful with the longer 1000-2000m intervals. If you run these too intensively along with racing regularly, you may find your form reduces. I would also advise you to not do any hard anaerobic sessions when racing regularly either, although 800-1500m runners could do some faster strides (2-3x150m) a few days before a race.

Tapering

Added to the advice in the previous paragraph: when you are in good shape and want to peak for a key race, don't hesitate to taper and reduce your training. Don't do any long, hard sessions in the last 10 days before the race and if you are normally running almost every day, you can add a rest day in the week before. I would also suggest to consider reducing the quantity of your training a bit and during the last two days you can reduce even more. For runners training 2-4 times a week: you probably will not need any further reduction as most will already have two days full rest before a race anyway. You can reduce the quantity of your sessions slightly in the final week though, to freshen up your legs.

Tip: don't do anything unusual during the last 2-3 days before a race like a long bicycle ride, many hours of shopping, or a long walk.

What do you do the day after a race?

Naturally, this depends on how often you train. For runners training five times a week or less, the day after a 5-10km race can be a rest day with no training. If you train every day and are stiff and sore, it might be beneficial to have a very easy day after such a race. The traditional advice is an easy recovery run, but I would advise you do a very relaxed interval session such as 6x400m or 4x1000m. Most runners find that the slightly quicker running actually makes their legs feel better and recover faster, compared to just jogging for 30 minutes. But obviously, if after the warm-up your muscles feel like they can't endure any fast running, it's better to stop and go home. After a (half) marathon you shouldn't run at all for the following couple of days.

Crash training

For runners who are racing shorter distances (800-1500m), the day after a race could include a very heavy session. Successful 'easy interval' coach Lex Van Eck van der Sluijs often plans hard, mixed training sessions on Monday after a Sunday race. This is for when his athletes are in racing season and so it gives them five days to recover for their next race the following weekend.

During winter training I would do things the other way round. We would often have a hard, mixed session on Saturday, followed by a low key cross-country race on Sunday. These back-to-back harder efforts can give a great training stimulus for well-trained runners and are often called crash training. The important part is to have long recovery periods after these two heavy sessions.

You can't get into good shape: train less or more?

If you have been training diligently but you are not racing as you had hoped, then you need to consider whether you need something extra. Depending on the distance you are racing at, some athletes might need a few harder anaerobic sessions to get them into race shape; others may just need a faster endurance run. However, things can be completely opposite: you might be slightly tired or overtrained. I experienced this myself: I felt okay in training, but after a few minutes in a race I didn't feel the normal power, the normal freshness in my legs. Scaling back your training load and not racing is the only solution. Running less and/ or more relaxed, may increase your fitness more than adding extra sessions and forcing things too much. Go back to the basic programme of easy intervals over 200, 400 and 1000m, but run them a bit slower than usual.

Always warm-up, cooling-down is less important

Before every workout - even an endurance run - it is important to warm up: 10-15 minutes jogging followed by some mild, dynamic stretching and a few strides to finish should get your body prepared to train. Twice a week I would recommend you do a core stability programme along with some hopping and bounding exercises to improve your reactivity and running economy.

Recent insights suggest that cooling down is less important and after an aerobic workout or endurance run a bit of walking and a few light, dynamic stretches should suffice. That is not to say that cooling-down is bad for you, but if you are short on time I would suggest you do a thorough warm-up and skip the cool-down. However, after a hard anaerobic session I would advocate at least 10 minutes jogging or running at an easy pace to help the body get rid of any acidification in an active way, which could also benefit your aerobic and anaerobic system.

Anaerobic training in the Easy Interval Method

Although anaerobic tempos can be quite effective for improving your so called VO2max (maximum oxygen intake) and is necessary for well-trained middle-distance runners, experience has taught me that runners who train according to the Easy Interval Method do not need as much anaerobic training as those training in a more 'traditional' way. This is due to fact that when training in a mostly steady-state way, a runner must use the harder, anaerobic sessions to actually get used to running at faster paces again. However, when using the Easy Interval Method, a runner is already much more adept at running faster paces.

Who should do anaerobic training?

This very much depends on the type of runner you are and which distance you focus on, but to start with: my experience is that the average athlete running distances of 10km and longer doesn't need to do any specific anaerobic training. Just doing their easy interval training alongside races and/or some fast endurance runs with surges will be enough. Even more: anaerobic training could be counterproductive. Here are some rough guidelines:

Young runners

Advice for young runners has been given in chapter 5.4.

Novice runner

I wouldn't advocate any specific anaerobic training at all during the first 1-2 years of running. Doing your easy interval training plus a race or endurance run (for 5-10km runners) with surges (and also a fast 2-3 minutes at the end now and then) at the weekend will be enough to progress for these first 1-2 years. Even if you are a novice track runner focussing on 800 tot 3000m: refrain from any specific anaerobic training in the first year and still only small amounts in the second. Focus on your aerobic development, running economy and some speed.

Recreational runner

If you are a recreational runner (running 5-15km or more), you shouldn't worry about anaerobic tempos. Doing some easy interval training and a race or endurance run with surges at the weekend is enough. Even a simple and relatively light schedule will improve aerobic endurance, reactive strength and running economy and hence will probably lead to more enjoyable running, still with improved race times.

Average competitive middle-distance runner

If you have been running for 1-2 years already, have a reasonably strong aerobic base and your goal is to improve your personal bests at distances from 1500 to 5000m, then you can add some anaerobic sessions to your training. For athletes doing 3-4 sessions a week: do these anaerobic workouts during a pre-race build-up period of 6-8 weeks and just once every two weeks or 10 days. The frequency of your anaerobic workouts will depend on your fitness, training frequency and race schedule, because anaerobic workouts will be at the expense of other effective sessions. When you are racing weekly, your middle-distance races will function as your anaerobic effort. However, for 800m runners doing 3-4 sessions a week things are slightly different. During a pre-race period, they can have a short anaerobic workout every week. For serious middle-distance runners with five or more weekly sessions: you can do one anaerobic session every week for 6-8 weeks during a pre-race build-up period.

I recommend doing anaerobic tempos during a mixed training session which also includes speed work, aerobic intervals and perhaps some hill training. However, it can also be a separate anaerobic workout or a short anaerobic session before or after a shortened easy interval session.

Elite and world-class runners

Elite and world class-runners can do a weekly anaerobic workout in a pre-race preparation period and can even consider adding one extra occasionally. These top runners recover better than most and so their body can cope better with two carefully selected anaerobic workouts during a few weeks without races. World class runners will also do anaerobic training for half marathon and even for marathon.

For how many weeks/months should you do anaerobic training?

Every runner will respond differently to anaerobic training, so it is very difficult to prescribe an exact amount of time an athlete should spend doing these sessions. Previous training can have a huge effect and so each runner will have to experiment a bit in order to find out how much they need and how they respond. Experienced athletes will probably adapt quickly (their muscles already 'know' what to do) and may only need 3-4 anaerobic sessions and a few races and they will be ready for their key race. Others may need twice as much of this type of training to reach top form. My general advice would be to err on the side of caution when it comes to these very hard sessions. It is better to be slightly undercooked than to overdo things and end up overtrained.

Keep things in balance

Extending certain sessions or adding new sessions into your training can have a sudden and positive impact in your running which results in a step forward. Do not make the mistake of assuming that this one element is your 'golden' session and continue to keep adding more and more of the same at the expense of other sessions. For example, suppose you make good progress after adding 100m repeats into your schedule. There is a good chance you were lacking reactivity and power, and the 100m's 'cured' this. This is great, but do not keep adding more and more 100m's straight away. Keeping them in your schedule is important, but you will continue to grow and improve for maybe a year with this new stimulus. Only after a year or so - longer if you are still improving - should you considering adding more, but do not overdo it. Try to keep your schedule in balance with recovery and other elements of your program.

It is the same with double runs. These can often give a runner a sharp increase in fitness and so the temptation is to add more or run them faster. I made this mistake as I mentioned in chapter 3. Initially I ran my morning 10km runs in about 36-37 minutes and performed well. This new impetus led me to push the pace on these morning runs to the point where I was regularly running my morning 10km in about 33-34 minutes (and still racing at the weekend). It didn't take too long for me to lose my form and I started to feel tired and even got injured. If you do start feeling overly tired I would suggest you always go back to the basic training of the relaxed intervals and get fit again. When you re-introduce your morning runs, focus on keeping the pace very relaxed. Double runs can provide an excellent stimulus to improve performance, but they are also another strain on the body, so they must be implemented carefully.

It's also important to keep in mind that what works for a couple of months may not work forever. For example, a weekly anaerobic session may do wonders for your fitness for 6-8 weeks, but then your form may drop rapidly as you continue to include them. Or a heavy workout and training load may make you strong and fit during a build-up period, but could cause you to overtrain when you start running races. If this happens to you, I would always suggest you go back to the relaxed basic training of the Easy Interval Method.

Learn the easy interval running feeling

To begin with, I would advise you run your basic easy intervals at the suggested paces and distances, but I would urge you to focus on how your body feels at each pace and try to develop an 'easy-interval-feeling'. This will take some practice, but once you are in tune with the correct feeling it will enable you to run the intervals in more varied places where you can go by your watch and feel, as opposed to a track or marked course.

I would also urge you to listen to your body in regards to how it responds to the schedules and training paces in this book. Not every runner will respond the same to each aspect of the ideas suggested here. Some can do no endurance runs and perform well with only frequently racing at the weekend; others will need more. Some runners may thrive on doing 8x1000m easy interval training, whereas others will do 4x1000m and feel they have had enough. Whatever works for you, just let the basis of your programme be easy interval training; it works!

7.2 Example of a mixed workout

A mixed training session in the Easy Interval Method is a unique workout. When it is overseen by a coach, a runner will not be told beforehand what the exact session will be. A mixed session includes a random mix of sprints, hill runs, aerobic and anaerobic intervals, interspersed with walking recoveries and various all-body exercises. Under my coach Verheul every mixed training session was different, although a few aspects were nearly always included – two laps of 800m to finish the session was his personal favourite. Such sessions are greatly influenced by the surroundings that you are running in. My sessions were often done on mainly flat, fast trails with a few hillier trails included. Unfortunately, Holland is a very flat country and so our hill reps were never more than 40-60 metres in length.

The anaerobic component was emphasised only in the last months of our winter training and I never performed these sessions during a track season or if I was racing regularly. When I was racing every week (sometimes twice, such as 800 & 1500m or 1500 & 3000m) I would want to keep my training in between relatively light and as the races were anaerobic, including another hard session – such as these mixed workouts – would have been too much.

The anaerobic aspects of these sessions should only be done by reasonably well-trained runners and after a period of building a sound aerobic base.

Below I have given a real-life example of an average mixed session I used to perform. This would take me about 1:35-1:45hrs to complete. Such a session can be done in the last month of a preparation period and can be easily modified or shortened if required. During the beginning of your aerobic build-up phase you should focus more on the aerobic paces.

As I mentioned earlier, I believe that when you combine both anaerobic and aerobic tempos in the same session you will get a better training effect. You are teaching your body to break down the waste products in an active way and also giving your maximum oxygen uptake (VO2max) an extra boost.

The exercises referred to below can be chosen from your own repertoire or from the following: hops (ideally uphill), bounding, planks and other core stability exercises, sit-ups, push-ups and various types of crawling - forwards, backwards and even uphill! Think of it as similar to circuit training.

1.   10-12 minutes jogging to warm up.
2.   10 minutes of exercises, gentle, dynamic stretching and core stability; a few strides.
3.   4 minutes effort below the lactate threshold (at easy 1000m effort intensity or a bit slower), walk/jog 3-4 minutes.
4.   A small lap of 150-200m is repeated 3-6 times non-stop; 50-100m is run at almost full speed, with the recovery at an easy endurance pace. This can be done by a watch if required. Next 4 minutes walking/jogging as recovery, with another exercise included.
5.   1-2 reps of 700-800m at 10km race intensity; walk/jog 4-6 minutes and 1-2 exercises.
6.   4-5x 30 seconds at 1500m race intensity, with 1 minute easy recovery between the reps; walk/jog 4 minutes and 1 exercise.
7.   3-6 minutes on a hilly loop below your lactate threshold pace (at easy 1000m effort intensity or a bit slower); walk/jog 4 minutes.
8.   3x60m hill sprints with 1-2 minutes recovery between each effort; walk/jog 4 minutes.
9.   400m fast at 5km race intensity, immediately followed by 3 minutes easy over hilly terrain (although the intensity might feel moderate); walk/jog 4-6 minutes and an exercise.
10. 400-500m acceleration run where you increase the pace every 50m until you reach your maximum speed; 4-6 minutes recovery with 2 exercises.
11. 6 minutes over hilly terrain under your lactate threshold intensity (at easy 1000m effort intensity or a bit slower) but try to push the uphill sections a little bit harder; walk/jog 4 minutes.
12. 1600m non-stop, gradually increasing the pace each 400m. The first 400m is run at a fast endurance pace, the second at LT intensity, the third at 5-10km race intensity. The next 200m would be at 3-5km race intensity and the last 200m close to 1500m pace.
13. 5-10 minutes jogging, some gentle, dynamic stretching and you are done!

Wheel-barrow walk exercise during a mixed session in the forest. Photo: Klaas Lok

7.3 Example sets of anaerobic tempos

The following sessions are suggestions of anaerobic workouts and are not set in stone. Experienced, well-trained faster runners can do a higher number of repetitions than I have suggested. You can perform your anaerobic sessions within a mixed training session, as has just been described in chapter 7.2, or you could do them separately on a track. Another option would be to do them alongside your normal easy interval session. Complete half your normal session (e.g. 3x1000m or 5x400m), and then do one of the anaerobic sessions described below. Or first do the anaerobic session, have a few minutes rest and next do your half-sized normal session, but a bit slower than normal. Obviously, on the track you could also alternate a hard tempo and an easy tempo as in a mixed training session.

Try to run the longer, harder efforts at a gradually increasing speed as has been discussed in chapter 5.2 in the paragraph: 'How to run your hard, long anaerobic tempos'. You should refrain from going at your maximum effort. Remember the difference between race speed and race intensity as I discussed in chapter 5.2. These sessions will feel much harder than your normal basic easy interval sessions, but continue to focus on running as relaxed as possible with the feeling of a normal strong stride.

Feel free to combine some elements of the sessions to make it more fun or relevant to you and your race distance.

1. 2-3x1000m with 3 minutes rest (walking or jogging). The 1000's should be run around 5-10km race intensity (not race pace; this is applicable for all mentioned race intensities hereafter).
2. 1-2x(1000-400m) with 1-2 minutes rest between the 1000 and 400m. The 1000m should be at 5km race intensity with the 400m at a slightly faster pace. If you want to do the second set, implement a 5-10 minute jogging rest between sets.
3. 1x(2000-400m). Pace will be 5-10km race intensity with 1-2 minutes jog between intervals.
4. 1x(3000-400m). Pace around 10km race intensity with 1-2 minutes jog between intervals.
5. 2x1000m (or 1200m) progressing in speed. Start the first 200m at slower than your usual 1000m pace and accelerate every 200m until the final 200m is near to your 800m race pace. Have 5-10 minutes walking and jogging before starting your second tempo. You could also do this session using your watch and accelerate every 30 seconds for three minutes.
6. 400-300-200-100m with 100m jog between each tempo. The 400m should be at 3000m race intensity, the 300m at 1500m race intensity, the 200m at 800m race intensity and the final 100m almost maximum speed. Have 5-10 minutes walking and jogging and perhaps repeat.
7. 5-8x200m with 30 seconds jogging rest. Run the 200m's at 1500m race intensity. If you do not have a measured course you can just do 30 second efforts with 30 seconds jogging rest. Well-trained runners could go up to 10-15 repetitions.
8. Set of fast 50m's as described on page 57.
9. Run 2000m, alternating speed every 100m. The first 100m in 1500-800m race intensity and the second at moderate endurance run intensity.
10. Perform an almost 'random' mix of various lengths, speeds and intensities as described in chapter 7.2. I would suggest these are run on feel rather than run to the clock and perhaps best performed in a group under the guidance of a coach. If you do want a more solid structure, you could use the following example of a set: long tempo, short tempo, hills or sprints, followed by exercises.

7.4 Examples of race imitations

I would always advise competitive runners to have a few 'tune-up' races before their main goal race. Unfortunately, it may not always be possible to find a suitable race and in that situation I would advise using the following race imitation sessions to replace them. These are essentially time trials – if you have a teammate capable of pacing you for half the race distance that would be great.

Race imitation for 800m

You will run an 800m near to your race intensity, which means a handful of seconds slower than your best (assuming good conditions). Rest for about 30 minutes with some walking, jogging, stretching and then run 400m 3-4 seconds slower than your recent best time. Again, a teammate can pace you for 200m to make it easier.

Race imitation for 1500m

A 1500m runner can do a similar session over 1200 and 400m at near race intensity. Alternatively, I prefer a fast set of 1000-400m with just 1-2 minutes rest.

Race imitation for 3000m

For 3000m runners I would suggest a 1500m time trial or a set of 1500-400m with 1-2 minutes rest. The 1500m can be close to 3000m race intensity with the 400m a second per lap faster.

Race imitation for 5-10km

For runners targeting 5-10km races, a fast endurance run of 6-10km with one-minute surges at 10km race intensity can be performed as a race imitation session. Well-trained runners could combine this with an anaerobic session the day before like 2000-400m, as mentioned in example 3 in chapter 7.3.

Klaas Lok (306) wins Dutch 10,000m title in 1982 in a time of 28:37, Cor Lambregts (328) came in 2nd in 28:53. Photo: Theo van de Rakt

8. Example schedules for novice runner and 10km

Please familiarise yourself with the advice given in chapters 6 and 7 before selecting any of the following schedules in chapters 8.1 to 8.7. I start with a schedule for a novice runner. Next you will find example schedules for 10km, starting with 1-2 sessions a week, up to 7-8.

8.1 Schedule for novice runner

The starting point is that you are completely new to running. If you are reasonably trained thanks to doing another sport, then you can proceed by large steps through the beginning of this schedule. If you have put on weight, this may increase your risk for running-related injuries, so it would be wise to slim down a bit first before you start your running schedule. One of the things you could do is walking, which also helps to have your muscles already getting used to a movement that resembles running a little bit. Meanwhile it could be wise to have a medical check-up.

In the following example I assume that you are willing to run 2-3 times a week, so after each workout you can have two days of rest. These two days after each workout will greatly help you to recover from the latest workout and reduce your chance for injuries. Start with walking as a warm-up, 5 to 10 minutes. Do some mild dynamic stretching and a few core stability exercises. Jog 30 seconds, walk 3 minutes. Jog 30 seconds again and walk 3 minutes again. Repeat this a couple of times, until you get to 4-6 reps. Your cool-down is just a few minutes walking and some mild dynamic stretching.
Rest 2 or 3 days.
Repeat the above workout.
Rest 2 or 3 days and so on.
You will find that gradually the speed of your 30-second runs increases. The pace should feel like comfortably fast running, meanwhile having the feeling that you can maintain the same speed for another 3-4 minutes with the same ease. Expand the number of repetitions up to 10 in a couple of weeks.

After a few weeks or months, depending on your progress, once a week you change the 30-second runs into one-minute runs. Start with 5-6x1 minute and the rest period after each one minute run may be 4 to 6 minutes; some walking and jogging, just how you feel. A short walk of 10-20 seconds after and before the start of a repetition is mandatory: this gives some extra relaxation to your muscles, so your muscles will - hopefully - be optimally relaxed when you start the next faster run.

The next step could be to try running almost every other day: three times a week. Then your schedule may look like this.

Mo	Rest
Tu	10x30 sec, rest on feel 2-3 min
We	Rest
Th	5-6x1 min, rest on feel 4-6 min
Fr	Rest
Sa	Rest
Su	10x30 sec, rest on feel 2-3 min

When this is all going well, once a week you replace a 30-second workout by a workout with longer tempos of 3-4 minutes (three reps) or maybe you combine some 30-second reps with 1-2 of these longer reps. These longer reps have to be run at a pace slightly slower than lactate threshold pace (see chapter 4). As an everyday novice runner this could be around your 10km pace. Your rest period is 5-6 minutes jogging and some walking. When you feel like it, go for it and start with your first long run of 15-20 minutes. Don't forget to also include some warming-up for a long run.

Then your schedule could look like this:

	Week1	Week 2
Mo	Rest	Rest
Tu	12x30 sec, rest on feel 2-3 min	12x30 sec, rest on feel 2-3 min
We	Rest	Rest
Th	7-8x1 min, rest on feel 3-5 min	7-8x1 min, rest on feel 3-5 min
Fr	Rest	Rest
Sa	Rest	Rest
Su	4x3-4 min, rest on feel 5-6 min	Moderately fast endurance run 15-20 min

At this stage you include three sets of strides of 80-100m at the end of your warming-up. These relaxed strides will help you to gradually build some extra reactivity and speed.

In case you are a fan of more variety in your programme, you could choose to also do a mixed training, in which you run different tempos in one interval workout once a fortnight; e.g. a session of 4-3-2-1 and half a minute, all easy interval tempos.

After some months it is best to occasionally convert the timed runs into measured distances, in order to get a better control of your speed and learn the corresponding 'easy-interval-running-feeling'.

When the 15-20-minute runs are going well, it is time to extend the endurance run to 6-8km and next to run your first 5 or 10km race. When you feel you are used to training 2-3 times a week according to the last schedule, it is time to apply a schedule of a next chapter.

8.2   Schedule 10km - 2 sessions a week

This is a basic schedule for a runner aiming at 10km, who wants to run twice a week, including a race. Please read chapters 6 and 7, including the table in chapter 6. Training just twice weekly is not enough to train according to the Easy Interval Method, which is characterised by its typical easy interval sessions over 200, 400 and 1000m. But I have composed a schedule for you that may still work better than training with just steady-state runs.

Your first session

To begin with, I presume that you are used to running and don't have problems running 10km in a race. Choosing your first session can be simple: just run a race or a moderate to fast endurance run of 8-12km with surges. Run the endurance run at an effort you feel like doing: the basic speed might be moderate for the whole run or it might be fast. It might also progress from moderate to fast by the end. Every 6-7 minutes you accelerate to a higher pace for 30-60 seconds, as described in chapter 6. When you feel strong, you can run the last three minutes at your 5-10km race intensity. Afterwards you rest a couple of minutes with some walking and mild stretching. Then, if your muscles feel ok and you want to do a bit extra, you run 3x100m relaxed (not faster than your 200m easy interval speed). In between each effort you rest with a 100m walk.

When doing the endurance run with surges, you should first do a warm-up, which you conclude with 3-4 strides of 80 to 100m.

Two examples for your second session

1. You can do a combination workout with easy interval tempos as follows:
   - Warm-up: 12-15 minutes jogging, exercises (stretching, core stability) and some strides.
   - Run 1-2x2000m (or mile), rest is 6 minutes.
   - Run 1-2x1000m, rest is 4-6 minutes.
   - Run 2-3x400m, rest is 3 minutes.
   - Run 4-5x200m, rest is 1 minute.
   - Finish your workout with 3-5x100m just a bit faster than the 200m runs.

   Adjust the number of intervals according to your own insight and capabilities and feel free to compose your own combination of easy intervals over different lengths and speeds. Of course, it is not necessary to do a workout like this on the track: when your easy interval tempo feeling is good, you can do this workout on your favourite loop on the road or in the forest.

2. An alternative for this combination workout could be the following: run a moderately intensive endurance run of 6-10km with surges and conclude your workout with a short 5x200m easy interval session or some easy intervals like 400-200-100m. If you like both workouts 1 and 2 then you alternate them every other week.

If you are ever short on time and unable to train twice a week, make sure you are doing the endurance run with surges (or a race).

8.3   Schedule 10km - 3 sessions a week

The schedules in this chapter are meant for runners who have run regularly for some time, done some races and are ready to add some (extra) interval training to their schedule.

Running just three times a week is not enough to really apply the full Easy Interval Method principles - characterised by its typical sessions of 200, 400 and 1000m's. That being said, even doing just one or two interval sessions a week may have a positive effect on your fitness and race times.

On some days you have a choice of sessions which you can choose from depending on your fitness level. As well as the standard sessions, you can also perform a combination workout: 1-2x2000m, 1-2x1000m, 2-3x400m, 4-5x200m, 3-5x100m. These sessions can be useful when only training a few times a week, as you can hit different paces and distances in one session.

Two-week schedule

If you want to race regularly and like to keep things simple, the following two-week schedule can be used and repeated for several months.

	Week 1	Week 2
Mo	Rest	Rest
Tu	Rest	6x1000m + 3-5x100m
We	6x1000m (eventually without walking in the recovery) or 4x2000m; + 3-5x100m	Rest
Th	Rest	5x400 & 7x200m
Fr	Combination workout (see text)	Rest
Sa	Rest	Rest
Su	Moderate endurance run 8-12km w surges	Race 10km

Schedule with a build-up period

The following schedule is an example of an aerobic build-up period of approximately six weeks followed by a racing period. Feel free to vary the length of the build-up period to fit your race schedule.

This schedule is for runners who may feel they had stagnated and their aerobic system needs a boost. If you are new to the Easy Interval Method I'd advise a simpler schedule such as the two-week example mentioned before, as progress can be made for quite some time with such an approach. Before starting this build-up period you should be fit - if you have been injured or sick recently, repeating the basic easy interval schedule with just 1000, 400 and 200m's for a few weeks would be advisable first. Don't run many races in this build-up period and preferably don't exhaust yourself too much when racing.

The first two weeks are almost completely focused on your 1000m intervals to improve your aerobic system. These repetitions are the main building blocks of this program when only training three times a week. Meanwhile you keep your reactivity and running economy at a good level by regularly doing your strides and 3-5x100m (or more) before or at the end of the core of your workout.

	Week 1	Week 2
Mo	Rest	Rest
Tu	6x1000m	6x1000m
We	Rest	Rest
Th	6x1000m + 3-5x100m	6x1000m + 3-5x100m
Fr	Rest	Rest
Sa	Rest	Rest
Su	6x1000m + 3-5x100m	Moderate endurance run 8-12km w surges + 3-5x100m

Over the next couple of weeks you can add an extra endurance run with surges to improve your 10km stamina. You can also run some races and well-trained runners can add 2000m's in week 4 and after. The next four weeks may look like this:

	Week 3 (and 5)	Week 4 (and 6)
Mo	Rest	Rest
Tu	6x1000m (eventually without walking) or moderate endurance run with surges 8-12km; + 3-5x100m	6x1000m or 4x2000m + 3-5x100m
We	Rest	Rest
Th	6x1000m + 3-5x100m	6x1000m +3-5x100m
Fr	Rest	Rest
Sa	Rest	Rest
Su	Moderate endurance run 8-12km w surges	Race or fast endurance run 8-10km w surges

Race period

After six weeks of this type of training with one or two races under your belt, you can start adding a bit more speed to your schedule and start racing regularly. This schedule is similar to the previously mentioned two-week schedule, with just one difference: the moderate endurance run in the first week is changed to either a race or a fast endurance run. Your race period may look like this:

Mo	Rest	Rest
Tu	Rest	6x1000m + 3-5x100m
We	6x1000m (eventually without walking) or 4x2000m; + 3-5x100m	Rest
Th	Rest	5x400 & 7x200m
Fr	Combination workout (see page 82)	Rest
Sa	Rest	Rest
Su	Fast endurance run 8km w surges or race 10km If no race: once in 4 weeks it is moderate 8-12km	Race 10km

At this point, anaerobic tempos aren't particularly useful. When only training three days per week it is not worth sacrificing your aerobic workouts for anaerobic interval training. If you have a few years' running behind you and are eager for some anaerobic training, then you could run the last 3-5 minutes of your fast endurance runs very quickly. Do not do these harder efforts in the week before a race.

Klaas Lok with clubmate Joost Borm, racing in relaxed style in a regional cross-country race. Photo: Theo van de Rakt

8.4   Schedule 10km - 4 sessions a week

These schedules are aimed at runners who have run regularly for some time and performed some form of interval training and races. Depending on how you arrange your training and races I have given you the options of a simple two-week schedule or a schedule with a more focused aerobic build-up period before peaking for a specific race. Some days also have a choice of sessions which you can choose from depending on your fitness level. Well-trained runners can do the 2000m's. Feel free to move any workouts if you prefer to have more rest before or after a race.

Two-week schedule

If you want to race regularly and like to keep things simple, the following two-week schedule can be used and repeated for several months.

	Week 1	Week 2
Mo	Rest	Rest
Tu	10x400m (or combination 5x400 & 7x200m)	6x1000m + 3-5x100m
We	6x1000m or 4-5x2000m or moderate endurance run 8-12km with surges; + 3-5x100m	15x200m (or combination 5x400 & 7x200m)
Th	Rest	6x1000m + 3-5x100m
Fr	6x1000m + 3-5x100m	Rest
Sa	Rest	Rest
Su	Endurance run with surges + 3-5x100m; if you are fit and your race shape needs a boost do 8km fast, if you have run many races, it is better to choose the moderate run 10-12km	Race 10km

Schedule with a build-up period

The following schedule is an example of a build-up period of approximately six weeks followed by a racing period. Feel free to vary the length of the build-up period to fit your race schedule.

This schedule is for well-trained runners who may feel they have stagnated and their aerobic system needs a boost. Before starting this build-up period you should be fit and healthy - if you have been injured or sick recently, repeating the basic easy interval schedule with just 1000, 400 and 200m's for a few weeks would be advisable first. Don't run many races in this build-up period and preferably don't exhaust yourself too much when racing.

The first few weeks are focused on 1000m intervals to improve your aerobic system, with the first endurance run at the end of the second week. These 1000m repetitions are the main building block of the programme, but you also keep your reactivity and running economy at a good level by regularly doing your strides and a few times 3-5x100m (or more) before or at the end of the core of your workout. Well-trained runners can implement 2000m's after 2-3 weeks.

	Week 1	Week 2	Week 3
Mo	Rest	Rest	Rest
Tu	6x1000m +3-5x100m	6x1000m + 3-5x100m	6x1000m or 4-5x2000m + 3-5x100m
We	6x1000m	6x1000m	Rest
Th	Rest	Rest	6x1000m or moderate endurance run 10-12km w surges; + 3-5x100m
Fr	6x1000m + 3-5x100m	6x1000m + 3-5x100m	Rest
Sa	Rest	Rest	6x1000m
Su	6x1000m	Moderate endurance run 8-12km w surges	Moderate endurance run 10-12km w surges or race 10km

After about five weeks you shift your focus to a bit more speed by implementing one session a week of shorter intervals. As you are only running four times a week there isn't enough room to do two shorter sessions and so I suggest a combination workout of 5x400 and 7–8x200m.

At this point, any anaerobic tempos aren't particularly useful. When only training four days per week it is not worth sacrificing your aerobic workouts for anaerobic interval training. If you have a few years running behind you and are eager for some anaerobic training, then you could run the last 3-5 minutes of your fast endurance runs very quickly. Do not do these harder efforts in the week before a race. An example of weeks 6 and 7:

	Week 6	Week 7
Mo	Rest	Rest
Tu	6x1000m or 4-5x2000m or moderate endurance run 8-10km w surges; + 3-5x100m	6x1000m or 4-5x2000m; + 3-5x100m
We	Rest	6x1000m
Th	6x1000m + 3-5x100m	15x200m (or combination 5x400 & 7x200m)
Fr	Rest	Rest
Sa	10x400m (or combination 5x400 & 7x200m)	Rest
Su	Moderate endurance run 10-12km w surges + 3-5x100m	Fast endurance run 8-10km w surges or race 10km

Race period
During a racing period I suggest you skip any heavy workouts. If you run a race every other week, then you can apply the two-week schedule as described at the beginning of chapter 8.4. If you run a race every week, your schedule could be as illustrated below. Please remember what has been discussed in chapter 7.1: when running many races, make sure you run your intervals in a relaxed way.

Mo	Rest	Rest
Tu	10x400m or combination 5x400 & 7x200m	15x200m or combination 5x400 & 7x200m
We	6x1000m or 4-5x2000m; + 3x100m	6x1000m
Th	Rest	6x1000m + 3-5x100m
Fr	6x1000m +3-5x100m	Rest
Sa	Rest	Rest
Su	Race 5-10km	Key race 10km

After a period of up to three months with regular, almost weekly, racing I would advise an active rest as described in chapter 7.1. If you are targeting a few one-off races throughout the year as opposed to a strict racing season, then it is up to you how much rest you feel you need before building up again, but two weeks should be sufficient.

8.5   Schedule 10km - 5 sessions a week

The schedules in this chapter are meant for runners who have run regularly for some years, are comfortable with several interval sessions a week and running races regularly. Depending on how you arrange your training and races I have given you the options of a simple two-week schedule or a more focused aerobic build-up period before peaking for a specific race. Some days also have a choice of sessions which you can choose from depending on your fitness level. Well-trained runners can do the 2000m's. Feel free to move any session if you need more rest before or after a race.

Two-week schedule

If you want to race regularly and like to keep things simple - without targeting a key race - the following two-week schedule can be used and repeated for several months.

	Week 1	Week 2
Mo	Rest	Rest
Tu	6x1000m + 3-5x100m	6x1000m + 3-5x100m
We	15x200m	15x200m
Th	6x1000m or 4-5x2000m or moderate endurance 8-12km w surges; + 3-5x100m	6x1000m + 3-5x100m
Fr	10x400m	8x400m (extra easy because of the Sunday race)
Sa	Rest	Rest
Su	Endurance run w surges + 3-5x100m; if fit and your race shape needs a boost, do 8km fast; if you have run many races, better choose the moderate run 10-12km	Race 10km

Schedule with build-up period

The following schedule is an example with a build-up period of approximately six weeks followed by a racing period. Feel free to vary the length of the build-up period to fit your race schedule.

This schedule is aimed at well-trained runners who may feel like they have stagnated and that their aerobic system needs a boost. Before starting this build-up period you should be fit and healthy. If you have been injured or sick recently, repeating the basic easy interval schedule with just 1000, 400 and 200m's for a few weeks would be advisable first. Don't run many races in this build-up period and preferably don't exhaust yourself too much when racing.

The first few weeks are focused on 1000m intervals to improve your aerobic system, with the first endurance run at the end of the second week. These 1000m repetitions are the main building block of the programme, but you also keep your reactivity and running economy at a good level by regularly doing your strides and a few times 3-5x100m (or more) before or at the end of the core of your workout. Well-trained runners can implement 2000m's after 2-3 weeks. When running five times a week, there is not enough room for two shorter sessions and so during this build-up I advise doing a combination workout of 5x400 and 7-8x200m.

	Week 1	Week 2	Week 3
Mo	Rest	Rest	Rest
Tu	6x1000m + 3-5x100m	6x1000m or 4-5x2000m; + 3-5x100m	6x1000m
We	Combination 400 & 200m	Combination 400 & 200m	6x1000m or 4-5x2000m or moderate endurance run 10-12km w surges; + 3-5x100m
Th	6x1000m	6x1000m	Combination 400 & 200m
Fr	Rest	Rest	Rest
Sa	6x1000m + 3-5x100m	6x1000m	6x1000m
Su	6x1000m	Moderate endurance run 8-12km w surges + 3-5x100m	Moderate endurance run 10-12km w surges + 3-5x100m

After about five weeks, well-trained, fast runners can add a few anaerobic tempos to their shortened combined session. I would still advise these runners to do no more than three sessions with these added anaerobic tempos. For example, you could perform such a session in week 5, 6 and 8.

Below is an example of week 6 and 7.

	Week 6	Week 7
Mo	Rest	Rest
Tu	6x1000m or 4-5x2000m or moderate endurance run 8-10km w surges; 3-5x100m	6x1000m or 4-5x2000m; 3-5x100m
We	Combination 400 & 200m + optional a few anaerobic tempos	6x1000m
Th	6x1000m	Combination 400 & 200m + 3-5x100m
Fr	Rest	6x1000m
Sa	6x1000m	Rest
Su	Moderate endurance run 10-12km w surges + 3-5x100m	Race 10km

Race period

After this build-up period it is time for regular racing. If you run a race every other week you can apply the two-week schedule mentioned at the beginning of this chapter. If you are racing every week I would avoid all anaerobic aspects in your training and choose a light schedule as illustrated below. Please remember what was discussed in chapter 7.1: when running many races, make sure you perform your intervals in a very relaxed way.

Mo	Rest	Rest
Tu	6x1000m or 4-5x2000m; + 3x100m	6x1000m + 3-5x100m
We	15x200m	15x200m
Th	6x1000m + 3-5x100m	5x1000m + 3-5x100m
Fr	10x400m	8x400m extra easy
Sa	Rest	Rest
Su	Race 5 or 10km	Key race 10km

After a period of up to three months with regular, almost weekly, racing I would advise an active rest as described in chapter 7.1. If you are targeting a few one-off races throughout the year as opposed to a strict racing season, then it is up to you how much rest you feel you need before building up again, but two weeks should be sufficient.

8.6   Schedule 10km - 6 sessions a week

The schedules in this chapter are meant for runners who have run regularly for some years, are comfortable with several interval sessions a week and running races regularly.

When running six days a week I wouldn't advocate regularly cutting down the sessions from the prescribed number of repetitions - as discussed in chapter 7.1. I am of the opinion that if you find the regular sessions (10x400m, 6x1000m etc) too much, then you are probably not (yet) fit enough to cope with running six days a week and therefore it is better to choose the five sessions a week schedule.

Depending on how you arrange your training and races I have given you the options of a simple two-week schedule or a schedule with a more focused aerobic build-up period before peaking for a specific race. Some days also have a choice of sessions which you can choose from depending on your fitness level. Well-trained runners can do the 2000m's.

Two-week schedule
If you want to race regularly and like to keep things simple - without targeting a key race - the following two-week schedule can be used and repeated for several months.

	Week 1	Week 2
Mo	8-10x400m	10x400m
Tu	6x1000m	6x1000m + 3-5x100m
We	15x200m	15x200m
Th	6x1000m or 4-5x2000m or moderate endurance run 8-12km w surges; + 3-5x100m	6x1000m + 3-5x100m
Fr	6x1000m or 10x400m	10x400m (extra easy)
Sa	Rest	Rest
Su	Endurance run w surges + 3-5x100m; if fit and race shape needs a boost do 8km fast; if you have run many races, it is better to choose the moderate run 10-12km	Race 10km

Schedule with build-up period
The following schedule is an example with a build-up period of approximately six weeks followed by a racing period. Feel free to vary the length of the build-up period to fit your race schedule.

This schedule is aimed at well-trained runners who may feel like they have stagnated and that their aerobic system needs a boost. Before starting this build-up period you should be fit and healthy - if you have been injured or sick recently, repeating the basic easy interval schedule with just 1000's, 400s and 200's for a few weeks would be advisable first. Don't run many races in this build-up period and preferably don't exhaust yourself too much when racing.

The first few weeks are focused on 1000m intervals to improve your aerobic system, with the first endurance run at the end of the second week. These 1000m repetitions are the main building block of the program, but you also keep your reactivity and running economy at a good level by regularly doing your strides and a few times 3-5x100m (or more) before or at the end of the core of your workout. Well-trained runners can implement 2000m's after 2-3 weeks.

	Week 1	Week 2	Week 3
Mo	6x1000m	6x1000m	10x400m
Tu	6x1000m + 3-5x100m	6x1000m or 4-5x2000m; + 3-5x100m	6x1000m
We	15x200m	15x200m	6x1000m or 4-5x2000m or moderate endurance run 10-12km w surges; + 3-5x100m
Th	6x1000m + 3-5x100m	6x1000m + 3-5x100m	Rest
Fr	Rest	Rest	6x1000m
Sa	6x1000m	6x1000m	6x1000m+ 3-5x100m
Su	6x1000m	Moderate endurance run 8-12km w surges	Moderate endurance run 10-12km w surges

After about five weeks you shift your focus to more speed by including shorter, faster sessions as well as adding - for well-trained, faster runners only - a few anaerobic tempos, e.g. 2-3x1000m or 2000-400m (more examples in chapter 7.3). These can be done as part of a mixed workout (see chapter 7.2) or in combination with a reduced easy interval session. For 10km I would advise those runners to do no more than a total of 3-4 sessions with these added anaerobic tempos. Below is an example of week 6 and 7.

	Week 6	Week 7
Mo	10x400m	10x400m
Tu	6x1000m or 4-5x2000m or moderate endurance run 10-12km w surges; + 3-5x100m	Moderate endurance run 10-12km w surges + 3-5x100m
We	15x200m	6x1000m
Th	6x1000m	15x200m
Fr	Rest	6x1000m
Sa	Mixed workout with optional anaerobic tempos	Rest
Su	Moderate endurance run 10-12km w surges + 3-5x100m	Fast endurance run 8-10km w surges or race 10km

Race period

After this build-up period it is time for regular racing. If you run a race every other week you can apply the two-week schedule mentioned at the beginning of this chapter. If you are racing every week, I would avoid all anaerobic aspects in your training and choose a light schedule such as the following two weeks. Please remember what was discussed in chapter 7.1: when running many races, make sure you perform your intervals in a very relaxed way.

	Week 9	Week10
Mo	10x400m	8x400m extra easy
Tu	6x1000m or 4-5x2000m; + 3x100m	6x1000m + 3-5x100m
We	15x200m	15x200m
Th	6x1000m + 3-5x100m	5x1000m + 3-5x100m
Fr	10x400m	8x400m extra easy
Sa	Rest	Rest
Su	Race 5 or 10km	Key race 10km

After a period of up to three months with regular, almost weekly, racing I would advise a long active rest as described in chapter 7.1. If you are targeting a few one-off races throughout the year as opposed to a strict racing season, then it is up to you how much rest you feel you need before building up again, but two weeks should be sufficient.

Klaas Lok (no 209) wins the 1984 Dutch cross-country championships; his fifth title. 1984 Olympic 5000m athlete Stijn Jaspers (no 2) leads. and 1984 Olympic steeple chase runner Hans Koeleman runs in 2nd position. Second from the left is Adri Hartveld. Photo: Theo van de Rakt

8.7   Schedule 10km - 7-8 sessions a week

The schedules in this chapter are meant for very well-trained (competitive) runners who have run regularly for some years, are comfortable with many interval sessions a week, running races regularly and fit enough to have one or two double days. As stated in chapter 7.1, it is better to have a double day with one day off rather than perform a session every day. Also note that when running your 1000m's in the morning of a double day, run them a few seconds slower than you normally would. Runners who feel they need to train 9-10 (or more) sessions a week should - in consultation with their coach - examine what extra stimulus they require. Some runners may need more aerobic sessions; others may need extra reactivity training such as 25x100m.

You should make your own decisions regarding the frequency of training: 8 sessions every week, alternate 8 sessions one week with 7 the next, or maybe even alternate 8 and 6 sessions. The schedules in this chapter mostly involve 8 sessions weekly, with 7 sessions in a race week. If you want to cut down another week with 8 sessions, then you could choose to skip a morning workout, although taking an extra day off (skipping a one-session-day) is also a choice. If training 7-8 times a week, it is advisable to have a relative easy week on a regular basis. A principle that is often used by elite runners is taking one easy week after three hard weeks.

Depending on how you arrange your training and races I have given you the options of a simple two-week schedule or a more focused aerobic build-up period before peaking for a specific race. Some days also have a choice of sessions which you can choose from depending on your fitness level.

Two-week schedule

If you want to race regularly and like to keep things simple - without targeting a key race - the following two-week schedule can be used and repeated for several months. I give you an example with eight sessions in week 1 and seven sessions - including a race - in week 2.

	Week 1	Week 2
Mo	10x400m or 6x1000m or 4-5x2000m (extra easy after a race)	10x400m or 6x1000m or 4-5x2000m
Tu	Am: moderate endurance run 8-12km w surges or 6-8x1000m Pm: 10x400m + 3-5x100m	Am: moderate endurance run 8-10km w surges or 6-8x1000m Pm: 10x400m + 3-5x100m
We	6x1000m	15x200m
Th	Am: moderate endurance run 8-12km w surges Pm: 15x200m	6x1000m +3-5x100m
Fr	10x400m	8x400m
Sa	Rest	Rest
Su	Endurance run with surges + 3x100m; if fit and your race shape needs a boost do 8km fast; if you have run many races, better to choose the moderate run 10-12km	Race 10km

Of course you could opt for a three-week schedule similar to these two weeks, with 8-8-7 sessions and just one race at the end of these three weeks. In this instance I would suggest doing a fast 8-10km endurance run with surges one week prior to a race.

Schedule with build-up period

The following schedule is an example of a build-up period of approximately six weeks followed by a racing period. Feel free to vary the length of the build-up period to fit your race schedule.

This schedule is aimed at well-trained runners who may feel like they have stagnated and that their aerobic system needs a boost. Before starting this build-up period you should be fit and healthy - if you have been injured or sick recently, repeating the basic easy interval schedule with just 1000, 400 and 200m's for a few weeks would be advisable first. Don't run many races in this build-up period and preferably don't exhaust yourself too much when racing.

The first weeks are focused on 1000m intervals to improve your aerobic system, with the first endurance run at the end of the second week. These 1000m repetitions are the main building block of the programme, but you keep your reactivity and running economy at a good level by regularly doing your strides and a few 3-5x100m (or more) repeats before or at the end of the core of your workout.

	Week 1	Week 2	Week 3
Mo	6x1000m	6x1000m	6x1000m
Tu	6x1000m + 3-5x100m	Am: 6x1000m or 4x2000m Pm: 10x400m + 3-5x100m	Am: 6-8x1000m or 4-5x2000m Pm: 10x400m + 3-5x100m
We	6x1000m	6x1000m	6x1000m
Th	Am: 6x1000m Pm: 15x200m	Am: 6x1000m Pm: 15x200m	Am: Moderate endurance run 10-12km w surges Pm: 15x200m
Fr	Rest	Rest	Rest
Sa	6x1000m + 3-5x100m	6x1000m	6x1000m
Su	10x400m	Moderate endurance run 8-12km w surges + 3-5x100m	Moderate endurance run 10-12km w surges + 3-5x100m

After about five weeks you shift your focus to more speed by including shorter, faster sessions as well as - for faster runners - adding a few anaerobic tempos. These can be done as part of a mixed workout (see chapter 7.2) or in combination with a reduced easy interval session. For 10km I would advise runners preparing for a certain target race to do 3-4 sessions with these added anaerobic tempos. I would do no more than one anaerobic session a week and none in the week of the race. Below is an example of week 6 and 7.

	Week 6	Week 7
Mo	6x1000m or 4-5x2000m	6x1000m or 4-5x2000m
Tu	Am: moderate endurance run 10-12km w surges Pm: 10x400m + 3-5x100m	Am: moderate endurance run 8-10km w surges or 6-8x1000m Pm: 10x400m + 3-5x100m
We	6x1000m + 3-5x100m	15x200m
Th	Am: moderate endurance run 10-12km w surges Pm: 15x200m	6x1000m + 3-5x100m
Fr	Rest	Rest
Sa	Mixed workout with optional anaerobic tempos	Mixed workout with optional anaerobic tempos
Su	Moderate endurance run 10-12km w surges + 3-5x100m	Fast endurance run w surges 8-10km or race 10km

Race period

After this build-up period it is time for regular racing. If you run a race every other week you can apply the two-week schedule mentioned at the beginning of this chapter. If you are racing every week I would avoid all anaerobic aspects in your training and choose a lighter schedule such as is illustrated below. In the first week I planned the two double days straight after each other in order to have three light days before your race on Sunday, but of course you can change that. Please remember what was discussed in chapter 7.1: when running many races, make sure you perform your intervals in a very relaxed way.

Mo	10x400m or 6x1000m or 4-5x2000m	10x400m
Tu	Am: moderate endurance run 10-12km w surges Pm: 10x400m + 3-5x100m	Am: moderate endurance run 8-10km w surges or 6-8x1000m Pm: 10x400m + 3-5x100m
We	Am: 6-8x1000m Pm: 15x200m	15x200m
Th	6x1000m + 3-5x100m	6x1000m
Fr	10x400m	8x400m
Sa	Rest	Rest
Su	Race 10km	Key race 10km

After a period of up to three months with regular, almost weekly, racing I would advise a long active rest as described in chapter 7.1. If you are targeting a few one-off races throughout the year as opposed to a strict racing season, then it is up to you how much rest you feel you need before building up again, but two weeks should be sufficient.

9. Example schedules for 5km and 5000m track

Some readers might wonder: what is the difference between 5km and 5000m? Well, 5km is on the road, in a park or forest and the distance might not be exact. It might differ 10 to 50m, while a 5000m is run on a measured 400m track. The training may be different as well, due to the fact that most 5000m track runners also regularly run shorter track races like 1500 & 3000m. These athletes will have these races instead of an anaerobic workout.

Please familiarise yourself with the advice given in chapters 6 and 7 before selecting any schedule in the following chapters 9.1 to 9.6. In these schedules you will find some anaerobic workouts. In chapter 7.1 I already explained that not everybody should implement anaerobic tempos in their training, such as young, novice and recreational runners. Make sure to perform the easy intervals in the week of your key race a few seconds slower than normal.

9.1 Schedule 5km - 2 sessions a week

For runners only doing two sessions a week, a schedule for 5km can be the same as the 10km schedule. However, if you have been training consistently for some years and feel you could benefit from some specific training, you could choose to implement a few harder workouts in the last month before your 5km key race.

This could be a shorter, faster endurance run of around 6km with surges, including a hard final 3-5 minutes, a time trial over 5km, or a race. It could also mean a combination workout (see chapter 8.2) in which you replace some easy tempos with a set of (2000-400m) or (1000-400m) at 5km race intensity, with just 1-2 minutes rest between the two tempos. I would suggest a cautious approach, in which you do the harder sessions of (2000-400m) or (1000-400m) just twice before your target race. I would advise you only perform these sessions once a week, preferably not in a week when you have a race and never in the week of your key race.

9.2 Schedule 5km - 3 sessions a week

For the majority of runners performing three sessions a week, a schedule for 5km will be the same as the 10km schedule in chapter 8.3. However, if you have been training consistently for some years and feel you could benefit from some more specific training, you could choose to implement a few harder sessions during the last 4-6 weeks before your target race.

An example of such a workout could be a faster endurance run of around 6km with surges, including a hard final 3-5 minutes, a time trial over 5km, or a race. It could also be an easy interval combination workout (chapter 8.2.) in which you replace some of the easy tempos with a few anaerobic tempos.

The following schedule is a continuation of the schedules in chapter 8.3 - either after repeating the two-week schedule a couple of times or after an aerobic build-up. After training for six weeks according to your 10km schedule, you can follow the schedule below with your key race at the end of week 12. I have given you some anaerobic sessions in the schedules, but feel free to choose your own, using the examples in chapter 7.3. It is up to you to decide if you are fit enough to include anaerobic tempos every week or to take a more cautious approach, and only do run them once every two weeks.

	Week 7 (and 9)	**Week 8 (and 10)**
Mo	Rest	Rest
Tu	Combination workout (ch 8.2) with optional anaerobic tempos, e.g. 5-8x200m with 30 secs rest (ch 7.3)	Combination workout with optional anaerobic tempos, e.g. 1x(1000-400m) at 5km race intensity
We	Rest	Rest
Th	6x1000m + 3-5x100m	6x1000m + 3-5x100m
Fr	Rest	Rest
Sa	Rest	Rest
Su	Fast endurance run 6km w surges + 3-5x100m, or race 5-10km (don't race every week)	Fast endurance run 8-10km w surges + 3-5x100m, or race 5-10km

	Week 11	**Week 12**
Mo	Rest	Rest
Tu	Combination workout	6x1000m + 3-5x100m
We	Rest	Rest
Th	6x1000m + 3-5x100m	4x400 + 6x200m easy
Fr	Rest	Rest
Sa	2000-400m fast at 5km race intensity + 2-3x1000m easy + 3-5x100m or a race, eg 3km (Th and Sa can be exchanged)	Rest
Su	Rest	Key race 5km

9.3   Schedule 5km - 4 sessions a week

For the majority of runners performing four sessions a week, a schedule for 5km won't be too different to their 10km schedule. However, if you who have been training consistently for a few years and feel you could benefit from some more specific training you could choose to implement some harder sessions during the last 4-6 weeks before your key race.

The following example of a 5km schedule is a continuation of the 10km schedules in chapter 8.4 - either after repeating the two-week schedule a couple of times or after an aerobic build-up. After training for six weeks according to your 10km schedule, you can then follow the schedule below with your key race at the end of week 12.

I have given some anaerobic sessions, but feel free to compose your own, possibly based on the examples in chapter 7.3. If you plan to implement some harder sessions, it is up to you to decide if you are fit enough to include weekly anaerobic tempos or to take a more cautious approach and perform them once every two weeks.

	Week 7	Week 8
Mo	Rest	Rest
Tu	6x1000m + 3-5x100m	6x1000m + 3-5x100m
We	5-8x200m moderately anaerobic (see chapter 7.3) + 6x400m easy	1-2x(1000-400m) moderately anaerobic + 6-8x200m easy
Th	Rest	Rest
Fr	6x1000m + 3-5x100m	6x1000m + 3-5x100m
Sa	Rest	Rest
Su	Fast endurance run 8km w surges + 3-5x100m or race 5-10km (don't race every week)	Fast endurance run 6-8km w surges

	Week 9	Week 10
Mo	Rest	Rest
Tu	6x1000m + 3-5x100m	6x1000m + 3-5x100m
We	5-8x200m moderately anaerobic + 6x400m easy	2-3x1000m moderately anaerobic + 6-8x200m easy
Th	Rest	6x1000m + 3-5x100m (move to Fr, if no race at Su)
Fr	6x1000m + 3-5x100m	Rest
Sa	Rest	Rest
Su	Moderate endurance run 8km w surges + 3-5x100m	Fast endurance run 6km w surges or race 5-10km

	Week 11	Week 12
Mo	Rest	6x1000m + 3-5x100m
Tu	6x1000m + 3-5x100m	Rest
We	10x400m	15x200m
Th	6x1000m + 3-5x100m	8x400m + 3x100m
Fr	Rest	Rest
Sa	(2000-400m) fast, 5km race intensity + 2x1000m relaxed + 3-5x100m; or a race, e.g. 3km (Th and Sa can be exchanged)	Rest
Su	Rest	Key race 5km

9.4   Schedule 5km - 5 sessions a week

For the majority of runners performing five sessions a week, a schedule for 5km won't be too different to their 10km schedule. However, if you have been training consistently for a few years and feel you could benefit from some more specific training you could choose to implement some harder sessions during the last 4-6 weeks before your key race.

The following example of a 5km schedule is a continuation of the 10km schedules in chapter 8.5 - either after repeating the two-week schedule a couple of times or after an aerobic build-up period. After training for six weeks according to your 10km schedule, you can then follow the schedule below with your key race at the end of week 12.

I have given some anaerobic sessions, but feel free to compose your own, possibly based on the examples in chapter 7.3. If you plan to implement some harder sessions, it is up to you to decide if you are fit enough to include these on a weekly basis or to take a more cautious approach and perform them once every two weeks.

Track runner

If you are running track races occasionally, you can replace some anaerobic sessions with shorter races over 800-3000m (you could even choose to run two of these shorter races in one week). Running those races in the final weeks before your peak race will benefit your race form and finishing speed at 5000m.

	Week 7	Week 8
Mo	Rest	Rest
Tu	6x1000m + 3-5x100m	6x1000m + 3-5x100m
We	5-8x200m moderately anaerobic (see chapter 7.3) + 8x200m easy	1-2x(1000-400m) moderately anaerobic + 6-8x200m easy
Th	6x1000m + 3-5x100m	6x1000m + 3-5x100m
Fr	Rest	Rest
Sa	10x400m (always exchange Fr and Sa if race at Sunday)	10x400m
Su	Fast endurance run w surges 8km, or race 5-10km (don't race every week)	Fast endurance run w surges 6-8km

	Week 9	**Week 10**
Mo	Rest	Rest
Tu	6x1000m + 3-5x100m	6x1000m + 3-5x100m
We	5-8x200m moderately anaerobic + 8x200m easy	2-3x1000m moderately anaerobic + 6-8x200m easy
Th	6x1000m + 3-5x100m	6x1000m + 3-5x100m
Fr	Rest	Rest
Sa	10x400m	10x400m
Su	Fast endurance run w surges 6-8km, or race 5-10km	Fast endurance run w surges 6km, or race 5-10km

	Week 11	**Week 12**
Mo	Rest	6x1000m + 3-5x100m
Tu	6x1000m + 3-5x100m	Rest
We	15x200m	15x200m
Th	6x1000m + 3-5x100m	8x400m + 3x100m
Fr	Rest	Rest
Sa	(2000-400m) 5km race intensity + 2x1000m relaxed; or a race, e.g. 3km (Th and Sa can be exchanged)	Rest
Su	Rest	Key race 5km

9.5   Schedule 5km - 6 sessions weekly

The following example of a 5km schedule is a continuation of the 10km schedules in chapter 8.6 - either after repeating the two-week schedule a couple of times or after an aerobic build-up period. After training for six weeks according to your 10km schedule, you can then follow the schedule below with your key race at the end of week 12.

I have given some anaerobic sessions, mostly on Wednesday, but feel free to compose your own, possibly based on the examples in chapter 7.3. If you plan to implement these harder sessions, it is up to you to decide if you are fit enough to include these on a weekly basis or to take a more cautious approach and perform them once every two weeks.

For well-trained runners it can be beneficial to swap 1000 for 2000m intervals once every week or two.

Track runners

If you are running track races occasionally, you can replace some anaerobic sessions with shorter races over 800–3000m (you could even choose to run two of these shorter races in one week). Running those races in the final weeks before your peak race will benefit your race form and finishing speed at 5000m.

	Week 7	Week 8
Mo	10x400m	10x400m
Tu	6x1000m + 3-5x100m	6x1000m + 3-5x100m
We	5-8x200m moderately anaerobic (ch 7.3) + 8x200m easy	1-2x(1000-400m) moderately anaerobic + 6-8x200m easy
Th	6x1000m + 3-5x100m	6x1000m + 3-5x100m
Fr	10x400m	15x200m
Sa	Rest	Rest
Su	Fast endurance run with surges 8km, or race 5-10km (don't race every week)	Fast endurance run with surges 6-8km

	Week 9	Week 10
Mo	10x400m	10x400m
Tu	6x1000m + 3-5x100m	6x1000m + 3-5x100m
We	5-8x200m moderately anaerobic + 8x200m easy	2-3x1000m moderately anaerobic + 6-8x200m easy
Th	6x1000m + 3-5x100m	6x1000m + 3-5x100m
Fr	10x400m	15x200m
Sa	Rest	Rest
Su	Fast endurance run with surges 6-8km, or race 5-10km	Fast endurance run with surges 6km, or race 5-10km

	Week 11	Week 12
Mo	10x400m	10x400m
Tu	6x1000m + 3-5x100m	6x1000m + 3-5x100m
We	15x200m	15x200m
Th	6x1000m + 3-5x100m	4-5x1000m + 3x100m
Fr	10x400m	6-8x400m extra easy
Sa	(2000-400m) 5km race intensity + 2x1000m easy; or a race, e.g. 3km	Rest
Su	Rest	Key race 5km

9.6   Schedule 5000m track - 6 sessions a week

The following example is based on the assumption that you have been training for at least six weeks according to the 10km build-up schedule as described in chapter 8.6 but with fewer races and a few more anaerobic sessions. I would suggest you do not race more than once every three weeks during the build-up period.

Next, as a serious competitive track runner, you can pick up the schedule below with your key race at the end of week 12. In this 5000m schedule any anaerobic workouts are now replaced by races from 800-5000m. If you are not able to do a scheduled race, perform a short anaerobic workout as described in chapter 7.3, e.g. 10x200m fast with 30 seconds between the 200's, or another short combination. Which one you choose depends on the length of the race you haven't done: if you missed an 800-1500m, I would advise 10x200m; if you missed a 3000-5000m race, my advice would be to do a set of fast 1000's or a combination like 2000-400m.

For well-trained runners it can be beneficial to swap 1000 for 2000m intervals once every one or two weeks.

	Week 7	Week 8
Mo	15x200m	10x400m
Tu	6x1000m + 3-5x100m	6x1000m + 3-5x100m
We	10x400m	10x400m
Th	6x1000m + 3-5x100m	15x200m
Fr	15x200m	6x1000m + 3x100m
Sa	Rest	Rest
Su	Fast endurance run w surges 8km	Race 5000m 15-30secs slower than your max

	Week 9	Week 10
Mo	8-10x400m extra easy	15x200m
Tu	6x1000m	6x1000m + 3-5x100m
We	15x200m	15x200m
Th	6x1000m + 3-5x100m	6x1000m
Fr	10x400m	8x400m
Sa	Rest	Race 1500m
Su	Race 1500m (if possible run 2 races: 800-1500m)	6x1000m extra easy

	Week 11	Week 12
Mo	15x200m	8-10x400m extra easy
Tu	8x400m extra easy	6x1000m + 3-5x100m
We	Race 3000m	15x200m
Th	6x1000m extra easy	4-5x1000m + 3x100m
Fr	10x400m	6-8x400m extra easy
Sa	Rest	Rest
Su	Race 1500m	Key race 5000m

9.7   Schedule 5000m track - 7-8 sessions a week

The following example is based on the assumption that you have been training for at least six weeks according to the 10km build-up schedule as described in chapter 8.7 but with fewer races and a few more anaerobic sessions. I would suggest you do not race more than once every three weeks during the build-up period.

Next, as a serious competitive track runner, you can pick up the schedule below with your key race at the end of week 12. In this 5000m schedule any anaerobic workouts in week 8 and after are now replaced by races from 800-5000m. If you are not able to do a scheduled race, perform a short anaerobic workout as described in chapter 7.3, e.g. 10x200m fast with 30 seconds between the 200's, or another short combination session. Which one you choose depends on the length of the race you haven't done: if you missed an 800-1500m, I would advise 10x200m; if you missed a 3000-5000m race, my advice would be to do a set of fast 1000's or a combination like 2000-400m.

For well-trained runners it can be beneficial to swap 1000 for 2000m intervals once every week or two.

	Week 7	Week 8
Mo	15x200m	10x400m
Tu	Am: 6x1000m or moderate endur run 8-10km w surges Pm: 10x400m	Am: 6x1000m + 3-5x100m Pm: 15x200m
We	Am: 6x1000m Pm: 15x200m	Am: 6x1000m or moderate endur 8-10km run w surges Pm: 10x400m
Th	6x1000m + 3-5x100m	15x200m
Fr	Anaerobic workout (Fr-Su can be exchanged)	10x400m
Sa	Rest	Rest
Su	Fast endurance run 8km w surges + 3-5x100m	Race 5000m, 15-30 secs slower than your max

	Week 9	Week 10
Mo	8x400m extra easy	15x200m
Tu	Am: 6x1000m Pm: 10x400m	Am: 6x1000m + 3-5x100m Pm: 10x400m
We	Am: 6x1000m Pm: 15x200m	Am: 6x1000m Pm: 15x200m (or 13x200 + 2x200 fast at 800m pace)
Th	6x1000m + 3-5x100m	10x400m
Fr	10x400m	Rest
Sa	Rest	Race 1500m
Su	Race 1500m (if possible run two races: 800-1500m)	6x1000m

	Week 11	Week 12
Mo	15x200m extra easy	15x200m
Tu	Race 3000m	Am: 6x1000m + 3x100m Pm: 10x400m
We	Am: 6x1000m extra easy Pm: 10x400m	15x200m
Th	Am: 6x1000m + 3-5x100m Pm: 15x200m	5-6x1000m + 3x100m
Fr	10x400m	8x400m extra easy
Sa	Rest	Rest
Su	Race 1500m	Key race 5000m

Klaas Lok (302) in the leading group during the World Cross-Country Championships in Paris, 1980. English runners Nick Lees (24) on the right, and Nick Rose (2x) behind him. Behind Nick Rose runs Fernando Mamede, world record holder 10,000m in 1984.

10. Example schedules for 1500m track runners

The following chapters are aimed at competitive track runners, which is why you will find schedules from 5 up to 7-8 sessions a week. Please familiarise yourself with the advice given in chapters 6 and 7 before selecting any schedule in chapters 10.1 to 10.3.

In the final weeks before your key 1500m race I recommend you minimise the number of sessions of longer interval training (over 1000m). Nearly all examples in the following chapters have just one session of 1000m intervals in weeks 10 and 11 and in the final week there are none at all. Make sure to perform the easy intervals in week 12 a few seconds slower than normal: after the extra intensity in the weeks before, you will need to recover.

10.1 1500m track - 5 sessions a week

This example schedule is based on the assumption that you have been training for at least six weeks according to the 10km build-up schedule as described in chapter 8.5, but with fewer races and some extra anaerobic sessions. I would suggest you do not race more than once every three weeks during this build-up period. About two months before your key 1500m race your schedule may look like this.

Mo	Rest
Tu	6x1000m + 3-5x100m
We	Mixed session, e.g. similar to the one in ch 7.2, with anaerobic tempos
Th	6x1000m
Fr	15x200m or 10x400m (alternate every other week) or combination 5x400 & 7x200m; + 3x100m
Sa	Rest
Su	Cross-country or road race, or moderate endurance run w surges 8km + 3-5x100m

If you can cope with it, I recommend doing some extra 100m's in order to train your reactivity and running economy a bit more, e.g. during the Wednesday mixed session.

Next you can pick up the schedule below with your key race at the end of week 12. In this 1500m schedule after week 7 any anaerobic workouts are now replaced by races from 800-5000m. If you are not able to do a scheduled race, perform a short anaerobic workout as described in chapter 7.3, e.g. 10x200m fast with 30 seconds between the 200's, or another short combination workout. Which one you choose depends on the length of the race you haven't done: if you missed an 800 or 1500m, I would advise 10x200m; if you missed a 3000 or 5000m race, my advice would be to do a set of fast 1000's or a combination session such as 2000-400m.

	Week 7	Week 8
Mo	Rest	Rest
Tu	6x1000m + 3-5x100m	6x1000m + 3-5x100m
We	Combination 5x400 & 7x200m	15x200m
Th	6x1000m + 3-5x100m	6x1000m + 3-5x100m
Fr	Rest	10x400m
Sa	Mixed session, with anaerobic tempos	Rest
Su	Fast endurance run w surges 6km	Race 5000m 15-30 secs slower than your max

	Week 9	Week 10
Mo	Rest	Rest
Tu	6x1000m + 3-5x100m	6x1000m +3-5x100m
We	15x200m	15x200m
Th	6x1000m + 3-5x100m	8-10x400m + 3x100m
Fr	10x400m	Rest
Sa	Rest	Race 3000m
Su	Race 1500m (if possible run two races: 800-1500m)	6x1000m extra easy

	Week 11	Week 12
Mo	15x200m	Rest
Tu	Rest	15x200m
We	Race 1000m	8x400m
Th	6x1000m extra easy	12x200m easy, 1x150m fast at 800m pace
Fr	15x200m	6-8x400m extra easy
Sa	Rest	Rest
Su	Race 1500m	Key race 1500m

10.2   Schedule 1500m track - 6 sessions a week

The following example is based on the assumption that you have been training for at least six weeks according to the 10km build-up schedule as described in chapter 8.6 but with fewer races and a few more anaerobic sessions. I would suggest you do not race more than once every three weeks during this build-up period. About two months before your key 1500m race your schedule may look like this:

Mo	10x400m
Tu	6x1000m + 3-5x100m
We	Mixed session, e.g. similar to the one in ch 7.2, with anaerobic tempos
Th	6x1000m
Fr	15x200m + 3-5x100m
Sa	Rest
Su	Cross-country or road race, or moderate endurance run w surges 8km + 3-5x100m

If you can cope with it, I recommend doing some extra 100's in order to train your reactivity and running economy a bit more, e.g. during the Wednesday mixed session.

Next you can pick up the schedule below with your key race at the end of week 12. In this 1500m schedule after week 7 any anaerobic workouts are now replaced by races from 800-5000m. If you are not able to do a scheduled race, perform a short anaerobic workout as described in chapter 7.3, e.g. 10x200m fast with 30 seconds between the 200's or another short combination workout. Which one you choose depends on the length of the race you haven't done: if you missed an 800 or1500m, I would advise 10x200m; if you missed a 3000 or 5000m race, my advice would be to do a set of fast 1000's or a combination session such as 2000-400m.

	Week 7	**Week 8**
Mo	15x200m	15x200m
Tu	6x1000m + 3-5x100m	6x1000m + 3-5x100m
We	10x400m	15x200m
Th	6x1000m + 3-5x100m	6x1000m + 3x100m
Fr	Rest	10x400m
Sa	Mixed session, with anaerobic tempos	Rest
Su	Fast endurance run w surges 6km	Race 5000m, 15-30 secs slower than your max

	Week 9	**Week 10**
Mo	8-10x400m extra easy	15x200m
Tu	6x1000m + 3-5x100m	6x1000m +3-5x100m
We	15x200m	15x200m
Th	6x1000m + 3-5x100m	8-10x400m + 3x100m
Fr	10x400m	Rest
Sa	Rest	Race 3000m
Su	Race 1500m (if possible run 2 races: 800-1500m)	6x1000m extra easy

	Week 11	Week 12
Mo	15x200m	8x400m
Tu	8x400m	15x200m
We	Race 1000m	8x400m
Th	6x1000m extra easy	12x200m easy, 1x150m fast at 800m pace
Fr	15x200m	6-8x400m extra easy
Sa	Rest	Rest
Su	Race 1500m	Key race 1500m

10.3   Schedule 1500m track - 7-8 sessions a week

The following example is based on the assumption that you strive to perform 7-8 sessions weekly, but scale down the number of sessions to six in the week of your key race.

Furthermore, I assume you have been training for at least six weeks according to the 10km build-up schedule as described in chapter 8.7 but with fewer races and a few more anaerobic sessions. Occasionally, a morning session will be an endurance run with surges, but generally it will be a session of easy 1000's. A well-trained runner could choose to run 2000's every two weeks if they prefer. I would suggest you do not race more than once every three weeks during this build-up period. Around two months before your key 1500m race your schedule may look like this:

	Week 5	Week 6
Mo	6x1000m	10x400m
Tu	Am: moderate endurance run 8km w surges Pm: 10x400m + 3-5x100m	Am: 6x1000m Pm: 15x200m
We	15x200m	10x400m
Th	Am: 6x1000m Pm: 20-25x100m	Am: 6x1000m Pm: 20-25x100m
Fr	10x400m	15x200m
Sa	Rest	Rest
Su	Mixed session, with anaerobic tempos	Cross-country or road race or fast endurance run 8km w surges

Next you can pick up the schedule below with your key race at the end of week 12. In this 1500m schedule after week 7 any anaerobic workouts are now replaced by races from 800-5000m. If you are not able to do a scheduled race, perform a short anaerobic workout as described in chapter 7.3, e.g. 10x200m fast with 30 seconds between the 200's or another short combination session. Which one you choose depends on the length of the race you haven't done: if you missed an 800 or 1500m race, I would advise 10x200m; if you missed a 3000 or 5000m race, my advice would be to do a set of fast 1000's or a combination session such as 2000-400m.

	Week 7	Week 8
Mo	15x200m	15x200m
Tu	Am: 6x1000m Pm: 20-25x100m	Am: 6x1000m Pm: 20-25x100m
We	10x400m	10x400m
Th	Am: 6x1000m Pm: 15x200m	15x200m
Fr	Rest	6x1000m
Sa	Mixed session, with anaerobic tempos	Rest
Su	Fast endurance run w surges 6km	Race 5000m, 15-30 secs slower than your max

	Week 9	Week 10
Mo	8-10x400m extra easy	15x200m
Tu	6x1000m + 3x100m	Am: 6x1000m Pm: 20-25x100m
We	Am: 6x1000m Pm: 20-25x100m	15x200m
Th	15x200m	8-10x400m + 3x100m
Fr	10x400m	Rest
Sa	Rest	Race 3000m
Su	Race 1500m (if possible run 2 races: 800-1500m)	6x1000m extra easy

	Week 11	Week 12
Mo	15x200m	8x400m
Tu	8x400m	15x200m
We	Race 1000m	8x400m
Th	Am: 6x1000m Pm: 20-25x100m	12x200m easy, 1-2x200m fast at 800m pace
Fr	15x200m	6-8x400m extra easy
Sa	Rest	Rest
Su	Race 1500m	Key race 1500m

In this chapter I will discuss training schedules and ideas for 800m runners who are approaching the event from an endurance perspective such as 1500m or even 3000m. I emphasise that this chapter is not aimed at those runners who are the 400m-type 800m runner. Due to the fact that such a runner is also aiming at performing over 400m, they will do more speed and less aerobic training. However, they could cherry pick some ideas out of it.

I have already discussed how many distance runners make one or more of the following mistakes:
• too much steady-state training (especially during race season).
• too much and too heavy anaerobic training.
• anaerobic training too close to (peak) race.

These mistakes can be especially damaging to the performance of 800m runners, although obviously not for all: world records have been run and Olympic titles won by runners who had the right balance between slow and fast mileage and were wise to skip steady-state training in race season. Unfortunately, many 800m runners are not that 'lucky' and may never fulfil their potential; most train far too heavy, unaware that they could make their running life much easier with lower mileage and less hard anaerobic training.

A high-profile Dutch 800m runner who experienced this is Bram Som, European champion over 800m in 2006. In 1998, as an 18-year-old, he ran 1:48:36 and eight years later, in 2006, he ran his best: 1:43.45, a Dutch record. In those years his aerobic mileage consisted of up to four endurance runs a week as you can see in the following schedule. This schedule was published on the official website of the Dutch Athletics Union and was presented during a symposium 'The Power of Aerobic Volume' in 2008. In my opinion it seems that - as Bram Som stated himself - in those days he was training more like a 10km runner.

	Bram Som training - May	Bram Som race week - June
Mo	5x30m 10x100m 11.0 sec, flying start	Endurance run 45 min+ 10x30 sec
Tu	Easy to moderate endurance run 45 min + core stability	In forest 6x3 min fast; or track 6x800m 2:24-2:16, rest is 2 min
We	5x60m + 10x200m 26-24 sec, rest 2 min; 5x300m, rest is 2 min	Easy endurance run 45 min
Th	Easy to moderate endurance run + core-stability	5x60m + 6x200m 26-25 sec, rest is 2 min
Fr	3x(300-250-200m rec 2min) rest between sets is 3 min	Rest
Sa	Fast endurance run (marathon pace) + training for Vo2max: 6x850m off road	15 min jog, plyometric exercises, 5 coordination runs
Su	Easy endurance run 60 min	Race

Unfortunately, he had problems with this training load which resulted in injuries and even an operation in 2007. At the end of 2008 he changed to easy interval training, coached by my clubmate Ruben Jongkind. However, he was so injury prone that he could only perform four running sessions weekly. Despite this minimal training load, easy interval training still turned out to be a very good method for him which made his running life much easier. On a schedule with about one third of the mileage of his traditional schedule (and only about 60% of what I would recommend) within a year he managed to almost equal his best 800m performance (1:43.59) and even beat his best times over 400 (46.55), 1000 (2:17.01) and 1500m (3:42.75). Bram also experienced – as many other runners did – that his running felt more powerful and more relaxed.

Next you can read two weeks of Bram Som's new way of training, based on easy interval training and on a careful approach due to his injury-prone past, which sometimes forced him to do some of his aerobic training on a bicycle instead of doing easy 1000m's:

	Build-up week, 23 Feb - 1 March 2009	18 May - 24 May 2009
Mo	12x200m (38-35)	Core-stability + general strength + 15 min mild stretching + 1 hr bicycling
Tu	Rest	2x(100-150-200-250m) uphill at VO2max-intensity, rest between sets is 3 min walk
We	6x400m uphill (1:15-1:10)	Rest
Th	Core-stability + circuit-training	Track: 3x(400+200m) 400m in 68, 200m in 800m race speed (26 sec per 200m); rest = 200m jog; rest between sets is 3-5 min
Fr	4x1000m in 3:30	Travel to Morocco
Sa	Rest	800m Rabat - 3rd place in 1:45.31, qualification for WC Berlin (in which he finished 7th in the final, just 0.57 behind winner Mbulaeni Mulaudzi)
Su	Coordination runs + 8x100m 15 sec	90 min bicycling

Please note that Bram did not scale back his training for this race in Rabat.

Starting around 2016, Bram Som - together with my former clubmate Piet de Peuter - is coaching Olympic and world 1500m champion, Kenyan Faith Kipyegon.

As has been mentioned in this chapter, an 800m runner can be successful with a traditional training schedule in which they have a proper balance between slow and fast mileage, but unfortunately often things go awry in the following, repetitive manner:

A talented young runner of 17 has been training for a year, approximately three times per week. He runs a couple of races and he ends his season with an 800m time of 1:53. The next two years he extends his training to 4-5 times weekly and as a 19-year-old he runs

1:46.8. We tend to conclude we have a successful training approach and a successful coach. In the following years the mileage in his schedule is increased - endurance runs of 45 to even 60 minutes are included - as well as more and harder anaerobic workouts. Extra recovery runs in the morning are also considered to be needed.

As a 21-year-old he succeeds to lower his personal best by a few tenths of seconds, but unfortunately one year later things turn the wrong way and he struggles to break 1:47. However, his coach convinces him that all this mileage and hard training will lead him to have success the next year, so he keeps on training in the same way. Unfortunately, in the years after he struggles to find his top form. He feels like his last 200m is weaker, which makes him decide to do even faster anaerobic training... with worse results. This script is far from hypothetical: I have seen this happen to several talented 800m runners.

Bram Som, regaining form with easy interval training. Chasing world indoor champion Abubaker Kaki in the FBK Games (Hengelo, the Netherlands) of 2009. Kaki wins in 1:43.10, Som finishes 4th in 1:44.80 . In 4th position David Rudisha, Olympic champion 2012 & 2016, who finished 3rd in 1:43:53. No 54 is Amine Laalou (Morocco), 2nd in 1:43.36. Photo: Klaas Lok

It is my view that many coaches overestimate the aerobic aspect of the 800m race and are also wrong that this should be trained via steady-state training. These two assumptions lead to a wrong approach in which many runners and coaches are afraid to stop steady-state training during the racing season...

Then there is this general idea that an 800m runner should do steady-state training in order to cope with a three-day championships, where the runners have to run rounds to qualify for the final. I totally disagree with this. My experience is that a runner who is used to daily interval sessions can cope better with the load of three races during a tournament than someone whose training is based on steady-state training. The simple reason is that the muscles of the first runner are much better used to the repetitive load of race speed.

So - even more than for other distances - easy interval training and not steady-state training is the basic building block for 800m runners - remember the fast twitch 2 fibres! Furthermore, it is my opinion that six running sessions weekly is sufficient for most 800m runners. Elite runners could carefully try out extra sessions.

The following example provides some ideas on what a schedule for an 800m runner, based on easy interval training, might look like.

For all distances of 1500m and over I advise a build-up similar to a 10km runner, however, this does not apply for an 800m runner. They should only sparingly perform endurance runs and place a greater emphasis on maintaining their reactivity by running 100m's through all the year.

Because 800m runners don't need as much mileage (and some even can't tolerate much) as 1500m runners do, I explicitly mention the choice regarding the number of repetitions, e.g. (4-6x1000, 8-10x400, 12-15x200). Every 800m runner has to decide how much mileage they can 'digest'. Naturally, there is always the possibility to alternate heavy weeks by light weeks.

Apart from the running sessions in the next example, 800m runners should consider doing extra plyometric training (explosive jumps and hops). Please remember my earlier warning in chapter 5.1 - these carry a high risk of injury. For elite 800m runners I would also encourage some weight training but only during a build-up period. Close to and during race season they should preferably do regular sets of 100m's easy interval training. When you feel able to cope with it, I suggest you perform even more than in the following schedule.

Week in December

Mo	4-6x1000m
Tu	8-10x400m + 3-5x100m
We	4-6x1000m
Th	12x200m; alternated by 15x100m every other week
Fr	4-6x1000m
Sa	Rest
Su	XC race or moderate endurance run 6-8km w surges + 3-5x100m

Two weeks in February

Mo	8-10x400m	8-10x400m
Tu	4-6x1000m	4-6x1000m
We	15-20x100m	15-20x100m
Th	4-6x1000m	15x200m
Fr	Rest	4-6x1000m + 3-5x100m
Sa	Mixed session, with a few moderate anaerobic tempos + speed	Rest
Su	12-15x200m	Cross-country race or endurance run with surges 6-8km + 3x100m

Week in April

Mo	12-15x200m
Tu	4-6x1000m
We	20-25x100m
Th	4-6x1000m
Fr	8-10x400m + 5x100m
Sa	Rest
Su	Mixed session with anaerobic tempos

Next is an example schedule for the final six weeks before a key race. I assume that in the weeks before this period you have done around five mixed sessions with speed and anaerobic tempos, about once a week. The alternative extra tempos in week 7 and 9 should only be done by experienced runners with a good recovery.

	Week 7		Week 8
Mo	12-15x200m		15x200m
Tu	4-6x1000m		4-6x1000m
We	20x100m (or 15x100m + add a few anaerobic tempos like 5x200m at 1500m race intensity - 30sec recovery)		20x100m
Th	4-6x1000m		4-6x1000m
Fr	8-10x400m + 5x100m		6-8x400m + 3-5x100m
Sa	Rest		Rest
Su	Race 1500m		Race 800m

	Week 9		Week 10
Mo	12-15x200m		6-8x400m extra easy
Tu	4-6x1000m		12x200m
We	20x100m (alternative 15x100m + add a few tempos like in week 7; or 1 set 400-200m fast with 30sec rest)		4x1000m
Th	4-6x1000m		20x100m + 1x200m at almost 400m race speed
Fr	8x400m		6-8x400m
Sa	Rest		Rest
Su	Race 3000m (alternative: if possible 2 races 800-1500m; 2nd alternative: anaerobic session, e.g. 1000-400m, see ch 7.3)		Race 800 or 400m

	Week 11		Week 12
Mo	12x200m		12x200m
Tu	6-8x400m extra easy		6-8x400m
We	Race 1000m (if no race then anaerobic session like 5-8x(200m at 1500-m race intensity - 30sec rest)		15-20x100m
Th	20x100m		8-10x200m + 1x150m at almost 400m race speed
Fr	6-8x400m		4-6x400m extra easy
Sa	Rest		Rest
Su	Race 1500m; or race 800 & 400m at same day		Key race 800m

Please familiarise yourself with the advice given in chapters 6 and 7 before selecting any schedule in the following chapters.

I would generally only advise you to begin training for a half marathon if you have already been running for about two years and have run a few 10km races at least. Ideally, you would have just finished a period of training for and running 10km races, followed by a few weeks of relative rest. This will give you a good base of fitness to build on for your half-marathon training. The following example schedules presume that you have this 10km base fitness and are used to interval training.

You decide how long and how to build up the long run

The first thing you will probably notice in the schedule is that I give you a longer run of 14-18km every two weeks. Some people find the longer runs quite taxing, and they are probably best off to run a maximum of 14km. However, if you can cope easily with them I suggest you add an extra 2-3 longer runs during the 13-week preparation period. Please remember that these schedules are just examples and are not set in stone. I don't give details about how to build up the distance, such as 12km in week 1, then 14km in week 3 and so on. That is for you to decide: some runners may need such a build-up, while others are better able to cope with long runs and can immediately start with 18km in week 1.

In the schedules you will come across the term 'easy/moderate endurance run with surges' numerous times. This means that the basic speed of this run is between easy and moderate with a few surges thrown in, but you could run the last 15 mins at a slightly more moderate pace if you feel good. I would not recommend this every time, but maybe every couple of weeks or so.

All of the longer runs with surges can be changed into a more structured, relaxed interval run without walking if you prefer. For example a 'Zatopek' session of (400m moderate – 400m easy) or (400m moderate – 1000m easy). Many modern watches now have the facility to beep at a set distance, so you could easily set it up to beep at a certain point which indicates a change of pace. If you can't run a scheduled 10km race, than replace it with a fast endurance run of around 10km with surges.

A common trait amongst half-marathon runners is to perform longer intervals compared to their 10km schedule. Whilst this does make sense, it can come at the expense of their running economy. This is why I emphasise the importance of doing your strides during your warm-up along with the scheduled 200 and/or 400m intervals. If possible, I would also recommend you regularly run sets of 3-5x100m to improve your reactivity and running economy.

I would like to re-emphasise that these schedules are only examples and I have kept the number of repetitions the same, but feel free to add or reduce repetitions as I describe in chapter 7.1. After a half marathon I would advise at least two weeks of relative rest before re-starting full training again.

12.1 Schedule half marathon - 3 sessions a week

Please familiarise yourself with the general information at the beginning of chapter 12 before selecting the following schedule. I didn't schedule a relative rest week, which isn't necessary when having just three sessions a week.

	Week 1	Week 2
Mo	Rest	Rest
Tu	6x1000m + 3-5x100m	6x1000m + 3-5x100m
We	Rest	Rest
Th	6x1000m	6x1000m + 3-5x100m
Fr	Rest	Rest
Sa	Easy/moderate endurance run 14-18km w surges + 3x100m	Moderate endurance run 10km w surges
Su	Rest	Rest

	Week 3	Week 4
Mo	Rest	Rest
Tu	6x1000m + 3-5x100m	Combination 5x400 & 7x200m
We	Rest	Rest
Th	6x1000m	6x1000m + 3-5x100m
Fr	Rest	Rest
Sa	Easy/moderate endurance run 14-18km w surges + 3x100m	Moderate endurance run 10km w surges
Su	Rest	Rest

Week 5

Mo	Rest
Tu	6x1000m + 3-5x100m
We	Rest
Th	6x1000m
Fr	Rest
Sa	Easy/moderate endurance run 14-18km w surges + 3x100m
Su	Rest

Week 6

Mo	Rest
Tu	Combination 5x400 & 7x200m
We	Rest
Th	Moderate endurance run 10km w surges or 6x1000m without walking; + 3-5x100m
Fr	Rest
Sa	Rest
Su	Fast endurance run 10km w surges

Week 7

Mo	Rest
Tu	6x1000m
We	Rest
Th	6x1000m + 3-5x100m
Fr	Rest
Sa	Easy/moderate endurance run 14-18km w surges + 3x100m
Su	Rest

Week 8

Mo	Rest
Tu	Combination 5x400 & 7x200m
We	Rest
Th	Moderate endurance run 10km w surges or 6x1000m without walking; + 3-5x100m
Fr	Rest
Sa	Rest
Su	Race 10km

Week 9

Mo	Rest
Tu	6x1000m + 3-5x100m
We	Rest
Th	6x1000m
Fr	Rest
Sa	Easy/moderate endurance run w surges 14-18km + 3x100m
Su	Rest

Week 10

Mo	Rest
Tu	Combination 5x400 & 7x200m
We	Rest
Th	Moderate endurance run 10km w surges or 6x1000m without walking; + 3-5x100m
Fr	Rest
Sa	Rest
Su	Race 10km

Week 11

Mo	Rest
Tu	6x1000m
We	Rest
Th	6x1000m+ 3-5x100m
Fr	Rest
Sa	Easy/moderate endurance 14-18km run surges + 3x100m
Su	Rest

Week 12

Mo	Rest
Tu	Combination 5x400 & 7x200m
We	Rest
Th	Moderate endurance run 10km w surges or 6x1000m without walking; + 3-5x100m
Fr	Rest
Sa	Rest
Su	Race 10km, 1-3 mins slower than your max

Week 13

Mo	Rest
Tu	6x1000m + 3x100m
We	Rest
Th	Combination 4x400 & 6x200m
Fr	Rest
Sa	Rest
Su	Key half-marathon race

12.2   Schedule half marathon - 4 sessions

Please familiarise yourself with the general information at the beginning of chapter 12 before selecting the following schedule.

I have scheduled week 8 to be light but as there are already three rest days, this is probably not necessary for all runners.

	Week 1	**Week 2**
Mo	Rest	Rest
Tu	6x1000m	6x1000m (Tu can be moved to Th)
We	6x1000m + 3-5x100m	6x1000m + 3-5x100m
Th	Rest	Rest
Fr	6x1000m	6x1000m + 3-5x100m
Sa	Rest	Rest
Su	Easy/moderate endurance run 14-18km w surges + 3x100m	Moderate endurance run 10km w surges

	Week 3	**Week 4**
Mo	Rest	Rest
Tu	6x1000m	Combination 5x400 & 7x200m
We	6x1000m + 3-5x100m	6x1000m + 3-5x100m
Th	Rest	Rest
Fr	6x1000m	6x1000m + 3-5x100m
Sa	Rest	Rest
Su	Easy/moderate endurance run 14-18km w surges + 3x100m	Moderate endurance run 10km w surges

Week 5

Mo	Rest
Tu	Combination 5x400 & 7x200m
We	6x1000m
Th	Rest
Fr	6x1000m
Sa	Rest
Su	Easy/moderate endurance run 14-18km w surges + 3x100m

Week 6

Mo	Rest
Tu	Combination 5x400 & 7x200m
We	Moderate endurance run 10km w surges or 6x1000m without walking; + 3-5x100m
Th	Rest
Fr	6x1000m + 3-5x100m
Sa	Rest
Su	Fast endurance run 10km w surges

Week 7

Mo	Rest
Tu	Combination 5x400 & 7x200m
We	6x1000m + 3-5x100m
Th	Rest
Fr	6x1000m
Sa	Rest
Su	Easy/moderate endurance 14-18km w surges + 3x100m

Week 8

Mo	Rest
Tu	Combination 5x400 & 7x200m
We	4x1000m
Th	Rest
Fr	8x400m
Sa	Rest
Su	Race 10km

Week 9

Mo	Rest
Tu	Combination 5x400 & 7x200m
We	6x1000m
Th	Rest
Fr	6x1000m + 3-5x100m
Sa	Rest
Su	Easy/moderate endurance 14-18km w surges + 3x100m

Week 10

Mo	Rest
Tu	Combination 5x400 & 7x200m
We	Moderate endurance run 10km w surges or 6x1000m without walking; + 3-5x100m
Th	Rest
Fr	6x1000m + 3-5x100m
Sa	Rest
Su	Race 10km

Week 11

Mo	Rest
Tu	Combination 5x400 & 7x200m
We	6x1000m
Th	Rest
Fr	6x1000m+ 3-5x100m
Sa	Rest
Su	Easy/moderate endurance run 14-18km w surges + 3x100m

Week 12

Mo	Rest
Tu	Combination 5x400 & 7x200m
We	Moderate endurance run 10km w surges or 6x1000m without walking; + 3-5x100m
Th	Rest
Fr	6x1000m
Sa	Rest
Su	Race 10km, 1-3 mins slower than your max

Week 13

Mo	Rest
Tu	Combination 5x400 & 7x200m
We	6x1000m + 3x100m
Th	Rest
Fr	6x400m extra easy
Sa	Rest
Su	Key half-marathon race

12.3   Half marathon - 5 sessions a week

Please familiarise yourself with the general information at the beginning of chapter 12 before selecting the following schedule.

With five sessions a week you should incorporate a light week half way through your schedule. I have only planned four sessions in week 8 for this reason. An option for some runners could be to have a light week every other week in which they perform just four workouts. If you do then I suggest skipping a 1000m workout in week 2 and 4, and combining the 200 & 400m workouts in week 6, 10 and 12 into one session.

For well-trained runners it can be beneficial to swap 1000's for 2000m intervals once every week or two.

	Week 1	**Week 2**
Mo	6x1000m	Rest
Tu	6x1000m+ 3-5x100m	15x200m
We	Rest	6x1000m + 3-5x100m
Th	6x1000m	6x1000m
Fr	15x200m	6x1000m + 3-5x100m
Sa	Rest	Rest
Su	Easy/moderate endurance run 14-18km w surges + 3x100m	Moderate endurance run 10km w surges

	Week 3		**Week 4**
Mo	10x400m		Rest
Tu	6x1000m		15x200m
We	Rest		6x1000m + 3-5x100m
Th	6x1000m + 3-5x100m		6x1000m
Fr	6x1000m		6x1000m + 3-5x100m
Sa	Rest		Rest
Su	Easy/moderate endurance run w surges 14-18km + 3x100m		Moderate endurance run 10km w surges

	Week 5		**Week 6**
Mo	10x400m		Rest
Tu	6x1000m		15x200m
We	Rest		Moderate endurance run 10km w surges or 6x1000m without walking
Th	6x1000m + 3-5x100m		6x1000m + 3x100m
Fr	6x1000m		10x400m
Sa	Rest		Rest
Su	Easy/moderate endurance run w surges 14-18km + 3x100m		Fast endurance run 10km w surges

	Week 7		**Week 8**
Mo	Rest		Rest
Tu	6x1000m		15x200m
We	15x200m		4-6x1000m
Th	6x1000m + 3-5x100m		Rest
Fr	6x1000m		8-10x400m + 3x100m
Sa	Rest		Rest
Su	Easy/moderate endurance run w surges 14-18km + 3x100m		Race 10km

	Week 9		**Week 10**
Mo	8-10x400m		Rest
Tu	6x1000m +3-5x100m		15x200m
We	Rest		Moderate endurance run 10km w surges or 6x1000m without walking
Th	6x1000m		6x1000m + 3-5x100m
Fr	15x200m		8x400m
Sa	Rest		Rest
Su	Easy/moderate endurance run w surges 14-18km + 3x100m		Race 10km

	Week 11		**Week 12**
Mo	Rest	Mo	Rest
Tu	6x1000m	Tu	15x200m
We	15x200m	We	Moderate endurance run 10km w surges or 6x1000m without walking
Th	6x1000m + 3-5x100m	Th	6x1000m + 3-5x100m
Fr	10x400m	Fr	8x400m
Sa	Rest	Sa	Rest
Su	Easy/moderate endurance run w surges 14-18km + 3x100m	Su	Race 10km, 1-3 mins slower than your max

	Week 13
Mo	Rest
Tu	5x1000m
We	12x200m
Th	4x1000m + 3x100m
Fr	6-8x400m extra easy
Sa	Rest
Su	Key half-marathon race

12.4   Half marathon - 6 sessions a week

Please familiarise yourself with the general information in chapter 12 before selecting the following schedule.

With six sessions a week you should incorporate a light week half way through your schedule. I have only planned five shortened sessions in week 8 for this reason. An option for some runners could be to have a light week every other week in which they perform just five workouts. If you do then I suggest skipping a 1000m workout in week 2 and 4 and the Monday 400m session in week 6, 10 and 12. Another option could be changing Monday into a rest day after the Sunday long run and moving the skipped 400m workout to a midweek day (preferably Wednesday) as a second session.

It can be beneficial to swap the 1000's for 2000m intervals once every week or two. Elite runners could opt to have a total of 2-3 mixed sessions in the final month, in which they do a few anaerobic tempos.

	Week 1	Week 2
Mo	10x400m	10x400m
Tu	6x1000m + 3-5x100m	6x1000m + 3-5x100m
We	6x1000m	6x1000m
Th	15x200m	15x200m
Fr	6x1000m	6x1000m
Sa	Rest	Rest
Su	Easy/moderate endurance run 14-18km w surges + 3x100m	Moderate endurance run 10km w surges + 3-5x100m

	Week 3	Week 4
Mo	10x400m	10x400m
Tu	6x1000m + 3-5x100m	6x1000m + 3-5x100m
We	6x1000m	6x1000m
Th	15x200m	15x200m
Fr	6x1000m	6x1000m
Sa	Rest	Rest
Su	Easy/moderate endurance run 14-18km w surges + 3x100m	Moderate endurance run 10km w surges + 3-5x100m

	Week 5	Week 6
Mo	10x400m	10x400m
Tu	6x1000m + 3-5x100m	Moderate endurance run 10km w surges or 6x1000m without walking; + 3-5x100m
We	6x1000m	6x1000m + 3x100m
Th	15x200m	15x200m
Fr	6x1000m	8x400m extra easy
Sa	Rest	Rest
Su	Easy/moderate endurance run 14-18km w surges + 3x100m	Fast endurance run 10km w surges

	Week 7	Week 8
Mo	10x400m Rest	Rest
Tu	6x1000m + 3-5x100m	8x400m
We	6x1000m	4x1000m
Th	15x200m	12x200m
Fr	6x1000m	4x1000m
Sa	Rest	Rest
Su	Easy/moderate endurance run 14-18km w surges + 3x100m	Race 10km

	Week 9		**Week 10**
Mo	10x400m		10x400m
Tu	6x1000m + 3-5x100m		Moderate endurance run 10km w surges or 6x1000m without walking; + 3-5x100m
We	6x1000m		6x1000m + 3-5x100m
Th	15x200m		15x200m
Fr	6x1000m		8x400m
Sa	Rest		Rest
Su	Easy/moderate endurance 14-18km w surges + 3x100m		Race 10km

	Week 11		**Week 12**
Mo	10x400m		10x400m
Tu	6x1000m + 3-5x100m		Moderate endurance run 10km w surges or 6x1000m without walking; + 3-5x100m
We	6x1000m		6x1000m
Th	15x200m		15x200m
Fr	6x1000m		8x400m
Sa	Rest		Rest
Su	Easy/moderate endurance run 14-18km w surges + 3x100m		Race 10km, 1-3 mins slower than your max

	Week 13
Mo	Rest
Tu	5x1000m
We	12x200m
Th	4x1000m + 3x100m
Fr	6-8x400m extra easy
Sa	Rest
Su	Key half–marathon race

12.5   Half marathon - 7-8 sessions weekly

Please familiarise yourself with the general information in chapter 12 before selecting the following schedule.

The following schedule rotates a cycle of eight sessions a week, followed by seven sessions the next. Please feel free to skip a workout in order to make it a cycle of 7-7 or 8-6. This schedule is aimed at well-trained runners, which is why you will find a few more long runs which are actually extended interval sessions of 15-20x400m. These extended easy interval sessions - make sure to run them more relaxed then your normal 400m workouts - could be seen as a 'Zatopek-workout' as mentioned in the introduction in chapter 12. If 15-20x400m is too taxing, then I suggest limiting the number to 10-12x400m and extend the easy part to 600 or 800m.

With 7-8 sessions a week you should incorporate a light week half way through your schedule, which is why I planned fewer and shortened sessions in week 8 in this example schedule.

It can be beneficial to swap 1000's for 2000m intervals once every one or two weeks. Elite runners could opt to have a total of 2-3 mixed sessions in the final month, in which they do a few anaerobic tempos.

	Week 1	Week 2
Mo	10x400m	10x400m
Tu	Am: 6x1000m Pm: 15x200m	Am: 6x1000m Pm: 15x200m
We	6x1000m	10x400m
Th	Am: 6x1000m Pm: 10x400m	6x1000m + 3-5x100m
Fr	6x1000m + 3-5x100m	6x1000m
Sa	Rest	Rest
Su	Easy/moderate endurance run 16km w surges + 3x100m	Moderate endurance run 10km w surges + 3-5x100m

	Week 3	Week 4
Mo	10x400m	10x400m
Tu	Am: 6x1000m Pm: 15x200m	Am: 6x1000m Pm: 15x200m
We	6x1000m	15-20x400m extra easy, without walking
Th	Am: 6x1000m Pm: 15x200m	6x1000m + 3-5x100m
Fr	6x1000m + 3-5x100m	10x400m
Sa	Rest	Rest
Su	Easy/moderate endurance run 16-18km w surges + 3x100m	Moderate endurance run 10km w surges + 3-5x100m

	Week 5	Week 6
Mo	10x400m	10x400m
Tu	Am: 6x1000m Pm: 15x200m	Am: Moderate endurance run 10km w surges Pm: 15x200m
We	6x1000m	15-20x400m extra easy, without walking
Th	Am: 6x1000m Pm: 10x400m	6x1000m +3x100m
Fr	6x1000m + 3-5x100m	10x400m
Sa	Rest	Rest
Su	Easy/moderate endurance run 16-18km w surges + 3x100m	Fast endurance run 10km with surges

	Week 7	Week 8
Mo	8x400m	Rest
Tu	Am: 6x1000m Pm: 15x200m	8x400m
We	6x1000m	4x1000m
Th	Am: 6x1000m Pm: 15x200m	12x200m
Fr	6x1000m + 3-5x100m	4x1000m
Sa	Rest	Rest
Su	Easy/moderate endurance run 16-20 km w surges + 3x100m	Race 10km

	Week 9	week 10
Mo	10x400m	10x400m
Tu	Am: 6x1000m Pm: 15x200m	Am: Moderate endurance run 10km w surges Pm: 15x200m
We	6x1000m	15-20x400m extra easy, without walking
Th	Am: 6x1000m Pm: 10x400m	6x1000m + 3-5x100m
Fr	6x1000m	10x400m
Sa	Rest	Rest
Su	Easy/moderate endurance 16-18km w surges + 3x100m	Race 10km

	Week 11	Week 12
Mo	8x400m	10x400m
Tu	Am: 6x1000m Pm: 15x200m	Am: 6x1000m Pm: 15x200m
We	6x1000m	15-20x400m extra easy, without walking
Th	Am: 6x1000m Pm: 15x200m	5x1000m + 3-5x100m
Fr	6x1000m + 3x100m	8x400m
Sa	Rest	Rest
Su	Easy/moderate endurance run 16-18km w surges + 3x100m	Race 10km, 1-3 mins slower than your max

	Week 13
Mo	Rest
Tu	5x1000m
We	12x200m
Th	4x1000m + 3x100m
Fr	6-8x400m extra easy
Sa	Rest
Su	Key half-marathon race

Klaas Lok (414) finishes third in a 10km road race in the Netherlands in 1986; with elite Dutch runners (winner Tonnie Dirks - 408; Marti ten Kate - 404; Cor Lambregts - behind Lok) and Scottish marathon runner John Graham (no 427 – winner of the 1981 Rotterdam Marathon in 2:09:28). Photo: Cor Eberhard

Please familiarise yourself with the advice given in chapters 6 and 7 before selecting any of the schedules in the following chapters. I assume that you have a sound base for 10km as well as for half marathon, which means that in the last miles of a half marathon race you don't break down and you don't need to walk due to stiff muscles and/or exhaustion.

Whatever kind of marathon runner you are – a 10km runner who runs a marathon just once every two years, or a specialist frequently running this distance – my advice is you only start your marathon preparation when you are in good 10km shape, possibly after a period of focusing on 10km races (and maybe a half marathon), followed by a few weeks of relative rest.

Interval training is your basic training

It is no surprise that even for the marathon the basic easy interval training of 200, 400 and 1000m intervals can be used as your general training (alongside a 2-3 hour long run with surges, which will be discussed further on). Don't be afraid to use the slower times in the table from chapter 6, because due to the long distance runs of 20-35 km you probably won't always be as fresh as during your 10km training. 'Listen to your body' and train at a comfortable, relaxed pace. Well-trained runners could opt to skip the 10-20 seconds walk between the 400 or 1000m repetitions once a week.

Do your 200 and 400m interval training...

Many marathon runners tend to extend the length of their interval workouts (e.g. swap 200's for 1000's or even 2000's) compared to their 10km schedule, but that may come at a detriment to their running economy. That is why I would like to emphasise that it is important to do your strides in the warm-up, as well as to run the scheduled 200 and/or 400m's and if possible, a twice weekly set of relaxed 3-5x100m. Due to the need to compensate the longer endurance runs and assuming that you already have built a good aerobic base with your 10km training, I scheduled even more short interval training over 200 & 400m compared to some 10km schedules in chapter 8.

... but don't do too many repetitions

Another thing you should pay attention to is to not extend the number of short intervals too much. You are already performing your long run of 2-3 hours at least once every two weeks, hence an extra workout like 40x200m or 50x400m (like Zatopek did) will probably be too taxing; leave this to elite runners. If you really want to do such a workout, change your long run into a 2-3 hour relaxed interval training.

Stick to the normal length of your interval training

In some schedules that you can find on the internet you will notice that - apart from adding the 2-3 hour long run - the length of a certain interval workout is often extended.

For example, in the first week a workout consists of 1000m intervals, in the second week it is 1200m, next 1600m, up to even 3000m! You will also often see a normal 6x1000m workout being extended to 12x1000m. This seems logical, but for most runners I would not advise this: just stick to your normal basic easy interval training. Why? Well, because you are already implementing slow endurance runs of 20 to 35km which will make the total workload already heavier than normal. Extending other workouts is something I only advise to elite runners. For example, 2017 marathon world champion, Geoffrey Kirui, coached by my former clubmate Piet de Peuter, does 20x1000m.

Warning

Assuming you are not a fun runner who just wants to finish the marathon, but a runner who is aiming at running their best time over the distance, interval training should be in your schedule. However, please be aware of the following: with more interval training you will probably develop a higher basic cruising speed (in other words: you will be able to run a faster 10km). This will make the first part of a marathon feel easier, but when you are a beginner in marathon running you probably won't have developed enough stamina to maintain this speed during the second part. So make sure to restrain yourself after the gun goes off. 'The half-way point in a marathon is at 20 miles', as the famous saying goes.

Long endurance run (with surges) is essential

Alongside the basic easy interval training another corner stone in your marathon preparation is the long, easy endurance run of 20 to 30km (with surges). Faster runners may go up to 35km occasionally, and world-class runners up to 40-45km.

In the past it was thought you had to run slowly to train your fat-burning system, but nowadays we know that a long endurance run is not necessary for this. It is true that when you run slowly, in percentage terms, you will burn more fat than carbohydrate, but in absolute figures you will burn more fat when you do interval training. Still, you do need to run regularly for 2-3 hours non-stop in order to have your muscles getting used to the heavy task of running the marathon distance; but as you know by now: my advice is to add surges to this run. Most runners who do surges in their long runs and a set of relaxed 100m's afterwards report that when running the next days they feel fitter, less stiff, have less heavy legs and have more reactivity. The intensity of the basic speed is easy, with the surges of 30 seconds every 8-10 minutes just a bit faster, no more than moderate. It is fine if you feel more comfortable with an even slower basic pace, as long as you do your surges.

This long run with surges can be changed into a structured fartlek like a 'Zatopek-session' of 400-400m or 1000-1000m (only for well-trained runners, because the easy parts are shorter compared to when you do a surge every 8-10 minutes) or any mix of distances you enjoy doing (e.g. 400-1000m). As long as the total load of your workout is easy to cope with and has a mix of easy and moderate intervals.

You decide how long and how to build up the long run

In the example schedules you will regularly see 20-30km (sometimes 35). I leave it up to you to choose the distance. A very slow runner will cover far less distance than a faster runner in the same amount of time so they may opt for the lower option. I generally advise runners to go no longer than three hours in their long runs otherwise they will nearly have a marathon effort every other week. A faster runner will be much more likely to cover 30 or even 35km under three hours, so they can choose the longer option. Also, I don't give details about how to build up the distance, such as 25km in week 1, then 27km in week 3 and so on. That is for you to decide: some runners may need such a build-up, while others are better able to cope with long runs and can immediately start with 30km in week 1.

Just as with every workout you first do a complete warm-up, including stretching and a few strides.

You will notice that in most of the example schedules I include long runs of 20-35km just once every two weeks, but if you are able to easily cope with long distances, then I suggest you perform these runs every 10 days or even every week. Remember, the schedules in this book are just examples. If you perform long runs every week, then you need a relaxed week half way through your preparation period: for this week skip the long run. If you are running six times a week or more, I would suggest an even lighter week half way, in which you skip one or more workouts and/or shorten a few sessions.

You will find that every second week is a relatively light week due to the lack of the longer run. However, due to the load of the long run in marathon training being quite high, I also mention the possibility of skipping one session every other week. For example, the example schedule with four sessions could be merged into a schedule with the sequence of 4-3 weekly sessions.

You perform your last long run of more than two hours no closer than three weeks before marathon day. Experienced elite runners could opt for two weeks.

Don't perform your long run when you feel tired

If you start your long run and after a few miles you feel tired and sluggish, just stop it and change your workout into an easy interval session like 200 or 400m's and perform your long run on another day. Consider taking a day off after a long run. Be sure to monitor your recovery by being aware how your easy interval sessions are feeling. When you have some experience with easy interval training, you will quickly notice when you have 'heavy' legs. Of course you will have bad days, but you shouldn't have many of those consecutive after each other. After 3-4 days with 'heavy' legs, take a day off, go back to your basic easy interval program and get fit again before trying the long runs for your marathon preparation.

Make sure to do at least half of your mileage on the road. This will get your muscles used to the hard surface. Be patient and realise that it takes many years of marathon running before you have reached your personal top performance, relative to your mileage. It's a marathon, not a sprint!

After your marathon

Naturally, the question arises of what to do after you have run your marathon. First of all my advice would be not to run at all in the first week. I would even suggest you avoid any other taxing physical activity, but if you really feel like having your body doing something, then a short 15-20 minute walk every other day and maybe half an hour relaxed bicycle ride could be an option. For the next two weeks I suggest you perform less than half your normal training and - for runners who normally run every day - no more than every other day. After three weeks you can start to build up your training again and after four weeks you can train according to your normal 10km schedule. During the first weeks your focus should be slightly more geared towards the short interval training in order to get your running economy back to 10km level again. Don't run any races in the first month after your marathon.

Some final recommendations: don't run more than two marathons a year and preferably run your marathon in cool weather. If you plan to run another marathon later that year, I suggest you perform a long run of around 20-25km once every two or three weeks even in your '10km period'.

The training for marathon is an adventure and the marathon itself even more. In my opinion it would be better to change the distance to 30km, because the average human being is not built for running 26.2 miles. I know runners who have completely quit running due to the marathon, although I must admit that millions of people find a great satisfaction in completing this distance.

As usual, the schedules in the following chapters are examples with the standard number of repetitions and can be made lighter or heavier (the latter only for well-trained runners) as has been described in chapter 7.1. You can also run the intervals to time rather than strict measured courses if you prefer. After a bit of practice you should be able to 'feel' the correct pace. This can be very beneficial for the longer interval runs where some runners may find it boring to do a measured loop. If you can't run a scheduled 10km race, then replace it by a fast endurance run with surges.

13.1   Schedule marathon - 3 sessions a week

Please familiarise yourself with the general information in chapter 13 - especially about choosing the length of the long run - before selecting the following schedule. With just three sessions per week most runners won't need a relative rest week halfway. However, if you do, you could choose to make week 8 lighter. If you find the long runs to be too taxing, an option could be to change this example schedule into a 3-2 weekly cycle. If you do, then I would suggest that for any week you choose to be lighter than scheduled, you simply skip an interval workout.

	Week 1 (and 3 and 5)		Week 2 (and 4 and 6)
Mo	Rest		Rest
Tu	6x1000m + 3-5x100m		6x1000m + 3-5x100m
We	Rest		Rest
Th	6x1000m		6x1000m + 3-5x100m
Fr	Rest		Rest
Sa	Easy endurance run 20-30km w surges + 3x100m		Moderate endurance run 10km w surges
Su	Rest		Rest

	Week 7		Week 8
Mo	Rest		Rest
Tu	Moderate endurance run 10km w surges or 6x1000m without walking		Combination 5x400 & 7x200m
Wo	Rest		Rest
Th	6x1000m + 3-5x100m		6x1000m + 3-5x100m
Fr	Rest		Rest
Sa	Easy endurance run 20-35 km w surges + 3x100m		Rest
Su	Rest		Race 10km or fast endurance run 10km w surges

	Week 9		Week 10
Mo	Rest		Rest
Tu	Moderate endurance run 10km w surges or 6x1000m without walking		Combination 5x400 & 7x200m
We	Rest		Rest
Th	6x1000m + 3-5x100m		6x1000m + 3-5x100m
Fr	Rest		Rest
Sa	Easy endurance run 25-30km w surges + 3x100m		Rest
Su	Rest		Race half marathon, 4-8 mins slower than your max

Week 11

Mo	Rest
Tu	Rest
We	Combination 5x400 & 7x200m
Th	6x1000m
Fr	Rest
Sa	Easy endurance run 20-25kmw surges + 3x100m
Su	Rest

Week 12

Mo	Rest
Tu	Moderate endurance run 10km w surges or 6x1000m without walking; + 3-5x100m
We	Rest
Th	Combination 5x400 & 7x200m
Fr	Rest
Sa	Rest
Su	Race 10km, 1-3 mins slower than your max

Week 13

Mo	Rest
Tu	6x1000m + 3x100m
We	Rest
Th	Combination 5x400 & 7x200m
Fr	Rest
Sa	Rest
Su	Marathon

13.2   Schedule for marathon - 4 sessions a week

Please familiarise yourself with the general information in chapter 13 - especially about choosing the length of the long run - before selecting the following schedule. With just four sessions per week most runners won't need a relative rest week halfway. However, if you do, you could choose to make week 8 lighter. Also, if you find the long runs to be very taxing an option could be to change this example schedule into a 4-3 weekly cycle. If you do, then I would suggest that for any week you choose to be lighter than scheduled, you simply skip a 200 or 400m workout or combine these into one session of 5x400 & 7x200m.

Week 1 (and 3)

Mo	6x1000m
Tu	6x1000m + 3-5x100m
We	Rest
Th	6x1000m
Fr	Rest
Sa	Easy endurance run 20-30km w surges + 3x100m
Su	Rest

Week 2 (and 4)

Mo	Rest
Tu	10x400m
We	6x1000m + 3-5x100m
Th	15x200m
Fr	Rest
Sa	Moderate endurance run 10km w surges + 3-5x100m
Su	Rest

Week 5

Mo	Combination 5x400 & 7x200m
Tu	Moderate endurance run 10km w surges or 6x1000m without walking; + 3-5x100m
We	Rest
Th	6x1000m
Fr	Rest
Sa	Easy endurance run 25-30km w surges + 3x100m
Su	Rest

Week 6

Mo	Rest
Tu	10x400m
We	6x1000m + 3-5x100m
Th	15x200m
Fr	Rest
Sa	Moderate endurance run 10km w surges + 3-5x100m
Su	Rest

Week 7

Mo	Combination 5x400 & 7x200m
Tu	Moderate endurance run 10km w surges or 6x1000m without walking; + 3-5x100m
We	Rest
Th	6x1000m
Fr	Rest
Sa	Easy endurance run 20-35km w surges + 3x100m
Su	Rest

Week 8

Mo	Rest
Tu	10x400m
We	6x1000m + 3-5x100m
Th	15x200m
Fr	Rest
Sa	Rest
Su	Race 10km or fast endurance run 10km w surges

Week 9

Mo	Rest
Tu	Combination 5x400 & 7x200m
We	Moderate endurance run 10km w surges or 6x1000m without walking; + 3-5x100m
Th	6x1000m
Fr	Rest
Sa	Easy endurance run 25-30km w surges + 3x100m
Su	Rest

Week 10

Mo	Rest
Tu	10x400m
We	6x1000m + 3-5x100m
Th	15x200m
Fr	Rest
Sa	Rest
Su	Race half marathon, 4-8 mins slower than your max

Week 11

Mo	Rest
Tu	Rest
We	10x400m
Th	6x1000m + 3-5x100m
Fr	15x200m
Sa	Easy endurance run 20-25km w surges + 3x100m
Su	Rest

Week 12

Mo	Rest
Tu	6x1000m
We	Moderate endurance run 10km w surges or 6x1000m without walking; + 3-5x100m
Th	Rest
Fr	Combination 5x400 & 7x200m
Sa	Rest
Su	Race 10km, 1-3 mins slower than your max

Week 13

Mo	Rest
Tu	Combination 5x400 & 7x200m
We	6x1000m + 3x100m
Th	Rest
Fr	6x400m extra easy
Sa	Rest
Su	Marathon

13.3 Schedule marathon - 5 sessions a week

Please familiarise yourself with the general information in chapter 13 - especially about choosing the length of the long run - before selecting the following schedule. With five sessions it is wise to have a lighter week half way through your preparation. I have scheduled week 8 to only have four shortened sessions for this reason. However, if you find the long runs to be very taxing, an option could be to reduce the schedule by one session every other week. If you do, then I would suggest that for any week you choose to be lighter than scheduled, you simply skip a 200 or 400m workout or combine these into one session of 5x400 & 7x200m. Well-trained runners could choose to change a 1000m session into 2000m's once every one or two weeks.

	Week 1 (and 3)		**Week 2 (and 4)**
Mo	6x1000m	Rest	
Tu	6x1000m + 3-5x100m	8-10x400m	
We	Rest	6x1000m + 3-5x100m	
Th	6x1000m	6x1000m	
Fr	10x400m	15x200m	
Sa	Rest	Moderate endurance run 10km w surges + 3-5x100m	
Su	Easy endurance run w surges 20-30km + 3x100m	Rest	

	Week 5		**Week 6**
Mo	Combination 5x400 & 7x200m	Rest	
Tu	Moderate endurance run 10km w surges or 6x1000m without walking; + 3-5x100m	8-10x400m	
We	Rest	6x1000m + 3-5x100m	
Th	6x1000m	6x1000m	
Fr	6x1000m	15x200m	
Sa	Rest	Moderate endurance run 12-15km w surges + 3x100m	
Su	Easy endurance run w surges 20-30km + 3x100m	Rest	

Week 7

Mo	Combination 5x400 & 7x200m
Tu	Moderate endurance run 10km w surges or 6x1000m without walking; + 3-5x100m
We	Rest
Th	6x1000m
Fr	6x1000m
Sa	Rest
Su	Easy endurance run w surges 20-35km + 3x100m

Week 8

Mo	Rest
Tu	Rest
We	6x1000m + 3x100m
Th	12x200m
Fr	8x400m
Sa	Rest
Su	Race 10km or fast endurance run w surges

Week 9

Mo	Rest
Tu	10x400m
We	Moderate endurance run 10km w surges or 6x1000m without walking; + 3-5x100m
Th	6x1000m
Fr	6x1000m
Sa	Rest
Su	Easy endurance run w surges 20-30km + 3x100m

Week 10

Mo	Rest
Tu	8-10x400m
We	6x1000m + 3-5x100m
Th	6x1000m
Fr	15x200m extra easy
Sa	Rest
Su	Race half marathon, 4-8 mins slower than your max

Week 11

Mo	Rest
Tu	8x400m extra easy
We	6x1000m + 3-5x100m
Th	6x1000m
Fr	15x200m
Sa	Rest
Su	Easy endurance run w surges 20-30km + 3x100m

Week 12

Mo	Rest
Tu	8-10x400m
We	Moderate endurance run 10km w surges or 6x1000m without walking
Th	6x1000m + 3-5x100m
Fr	8-10x400m
Sa	Rest
Su	Race 10km, 1-3 mins slower than your max

Week 13

Mo	Rest
Tu	Combination 5x400 & 6x200m
We	6x1000m + 3x100m
Th	Rest
Fr	6x400m extra easy
Sa	Rest
Su	Marathon

13.4   Schedule marathon - 6 sessions a week

Please familiarise yourself with the general information in chapter 13 - especially about choosing the length of the long run - before selecting the following schedule. With six sessions it is wise to have a lighter week half way through your preparation. I have scheduled week 8 with five (mostly shortened) sessions for this reason. However, if you find the long runs to be very taxing an option could be to reduce the schedule by one session every other week. If you do, then I would suggest that for any week you choose to be lighter than scheduled, you simply skip a 200 or 400m workout or combine these into one session of 5x400 & 7x200m.

You will notice that on some Wednesday's I have scheduled two sessions in one day. This is to train your body to get used to some extra load and also gives you the possibility of having an extra day of rest. However, feel free to move the second workout to a 'rest' day elsewhere in that week if you wish. You could choose to change a 1000m session into 2000m's once every one or two weeks.

	Week 1	Week 2
Mo	6x1000m	Rest
Tu	15x200m	8-10x400m
We	6x1000m + 3-5x100m	Am: 6x1000m Pm: 15x200m
Th	6x1000m	6x1000m + 3-5x100m
Fr	10x400m	10x400m
Sa	Rest	Rest
Su	Easy endurance run 20-30km w surges + 3x100m	Moderate endurance run 10km w surges + 3x100m

	Week 3 (and 5)	Week 4 (and 6)
Mo	10x400m	Rest
Tu	6x1000m	8-10x400m
We	Moderate endurance run 10km w surges or 6x1000m without walking; + 3-5x100m	Am: 6x1000m Pm: 15x200m
Th	15x200m	6x1000m + 3-5x100m
Fr	6x1000m	10x400m
Sa	Rest	Rest
Su	Easy endurance run 20-30km w surges + 3x100m	Moderate endurance run 12-15km w surges + 3x100m

Week 7

Mo	10x400m
Tu	6x1000m
We	Moderate endurance run 10km w surges or 6x1000m without walking; + 3-5x100m
Th	15x200m
Fr	6x1000m
Sa	Rest
Su	Easy endurance run 20-35km w surges + 3x100m

Week 8

Mo	Rest
Tu	8-10x400m
We	6x1000m + 3-5x100m
Th	12x200m
Fr	8x400m
Sa	Rest
Su	Race 10km or fast endurance run 10km w surges

Week 9

Mo	Rest
Tu	10x400m
We	Moderate endurance run 10km w surges or 6x1000m without walking; + 3-5x100m
Th	15x200m
Fr	6x1000m
Sa	8x400m
Su	Easy endurance run 20-30km w surges + 3x100m

Week 10

Mo	Rest
Tu	8-10x400m
We	Am: 6x1000m, eventually without walking Pm: 15x200m
Th	6x1000m + 3-5x100m
Fr	8-10x400m extra easy
Sa	Rest
Su	Race half marathon, 4-8 mins slower than your max

Week 11

Mo	Rest
Tu	5x400m extra easy, or rest
We	10x400m
Th	6x1000m + 3-5x100m
Fr	6x1000m
Sa	15x200m
Su	Easy endurance run 20-30km w surges + 3x100m

Week 12

Mo	Rest
Tu	8-10x400m
We	Am: moderate endurance run 10km w surges Pm: 15x200m
Th	6x1000m + 3-5x100m
Fr	8x400m
Sa	Rest
Su	Race 10km, 1-3 mins slower than your max

Week 13

Mo	Rest
Tu	6x1000m
We	4-6x1000m + 3-5x100m, or rest
Th	12-15x200m
Fr	6x400m extra easy
Sa	Rest
Su	Marathon

13.5   Schedule marathon - 7-8 sessions a week

Please familiarise yourself with the general information in chapter 13 - especially about choosing the length of the long run - before selecting the following schedule. This schedule rotates a cycle of mostly eight sessions a week followed by seven sessions the next (with a few exceptions). Please feel free to skip a workout in order to make it a cycle of 7-7 or 8-6. If you do, then I would suggest that for any week you choose to be lighter than scheduled, you simply skip an interval workout. This example schedule is aimed at faster, well-trained runners who cope well with the long runs. That is why you will find a few more long runs, which are actually extended interval sessions of 15-20x400m. Make sure to run these more relaxed than your normal 400m workouts. They could be seen as a 'Zatopek-workout' as mentioned in the introduction in chapter 13. If the easy part of 400m feels too short, then I suggest extending it to 600 or 800m in order to make sure this run is not too intense.

Even with seven sessions a week I have scheduled two sessions in one day. This is to train your body to get used to some extra load and also gives you the possibility of having an extra day of rest. However, feel free to move the second workout to a 'rest' day elsewhere in that week if you wish. With 7-8 sessions you do need a lighter week half way through your preparation. I have scheduled week 8 with fewer and shortened sessions for this reason.

It could be beneficial to change the 1000 into 2000m intervals once every one or two weeks. World-class runners could implement a total of 3-4 mixed sessions in the final 5-6 weeks, in which they do a few anaerobic tempos.

	Week 1	Week 2
Mo	10x400m	Rest
Tu	Am: 6x1000m Pm: 15x200m	Am: 6x1000m Pm: 15x200m
We	6x1000m	10x400m
Th	Am: 6x1000m Pm: 10x400m + 3-5x100m	6x1000m + 3-5x100m
Fr	10x400m	6x1000m
Sa	Rest	10x400m
Su	Easy endurance run 30km w surges + 3x100m	Moderate endurance run 10km w surges + 3x100m

Week 3

Mo	10x400m
Tu	Am: 6x1000m Pm: 15x200m
We	Moderate endurance run 10km w surges + 3x100m
Th	Am: 6x1000m Pm: 15x200m
Fr	10x400m
Sa	Rest
Su	Easy endurance run 30km w surges + 3x100m

Week 4

Mo	Rest
Tu	Am: 6x1000m Pm: 15x200m
We	15-20x400m extra easy, without walking
Th	6x1000m + 3-5x100m
Fr	10x400m
Sa	6x1000m
Su	Moderate endurance run 10km w surges + 3x100m

Week 5

Mo	10x400m
Tu	Am: 6x1000m Pm: 15x200m
We	Moderate endurance run 10km w surges
Th	Am: 6x1000m Pm: 10x400m + 3-5x100m
Fr	10x400m
Sa	Rest
Su	Easy endurance run 30km w surges + 3x100m

Week 6

Mo	Rest
Tu	Am: 6x1000m Pm: 15x200m
We	15-20x400m extra easy, without walking
Th	6x1000m +3-5x100m
Fr	10x400m
Sa	Rest
Su	Moderate endurance run 12-15km w surges + 3x100m

Week 7

Mo	10x400m
Tu	Am: 6x1000m Pm: 15x200m
We	Moderate endurance run 10km w surges + 3x100m
Th	Am: 6x1000m Pm: 15x200m
Fr	10x400m
Sa	Rest
Su	Easy endurance run 30-35km w surges + 3x100m

Week 8

Mo	Rest
Tu	8x400m
We	6x1000m + 3-5x100m
Th	12x200m
Fr	4 x1000m
Sa	Rest
Su	Race 10km or fast endurance run 10km w surges

Week 9

Mo	8x400m
Tu	Am: 6x1000m Pm: 15x200m
We	Moderate endurance run 10km w surges
Th	Am: 6x1000m Pm: 10x400m + 3-5x100m
Fr	8x400m
Sa	Rest
Su	Easy endurance run 30km w surges + 3x100m

Week 10

Mo	Rest
Tu	Am: 6x1000m Pm: 15x200m
We	15-20x400m extra easy, without walking
Th	6x1000m + 3-5x100m
Fr	8x400m extra easy
Sa	Rest
Su	Race half marathon, 4-8 mins slower than your max

Week 11

Mo	Rest
Tu	8x400m extra easy
We	Am: 6x1000m Pm: 15x200m
Th	Am: 6x1000m Pm: 10x400m + 3-5x100m
Fr	6x1000m
Sa	Rest
Su	Easy endurance run 25-30km w surges + 3x100m

Week 12

Mo	Rest
Tu	Am: 6x1000m Pm: 15x200m
We	15-20x400m extra easy, without walking
Th	5x1000m + 3-5x100m
Fr	8x400m
Sa	Rest
Su	Race 10km, 1-3 mins slower than your max

Week 13

Mo	Rest
Tu	6x1000m
We	6x1000m + 3-5x100m
Th	12-15x200m
Fr	6x400m extra easy
Sa	Rest or 3-5x400m extra easy
Su	Marathon

This chapter looks at the different foot strikes that runners use and my opinion on what is the best technique for most runners. At the end I discuss how to hold your arms and more about your upper body.

Personally I classify three main types of foot strike: heel strike, flat foot strike and forefoot strike. Some of you will wonder why I don't discuss midfoot strike. Well, in my opinion, there is no such thing, as will be explained further on.

Heel strike

Advocates of heel striking have the argument - among others - that the ankle is a 'rolling joint' and therefore landing on your heel first is the most natural and best technique when running. This is certainly true when you walk, but not when you are a runner who is aiming to get the best out of themselves.

Heel strikers will also say that this technique reduces some of the strain placed on the Achilles tendon and calf muscles. This is true, especially for novice and heavier runners, however the overall impact forces are greater when heel striking, as I'll explain later.

In my definition, a real heel striker will capture the full impact of landing on the heel. During landing, the leg is relatively straight and the body's centre of gravity is located behind the landing foot. Even in the stance phase the latter is often true. This is not ideal for high speed development. When the foot lands in front of your centre of gravity you actually slow down your forward momentum a little bit during landing.

Flat foot strike

Most runners will - in some-way - be flat foot strikers:
- Some flat foot strikers will initially touch the surface with almost their complete sole which could result in a distinctive 'slapping' noise.
- Others might touch the ground first with their heel or with the lateral side of the sole, but immediately after, the complete sole makes contact with the ground.
- The largest group, however, seems to be what I call 'lazy' forefoot strikers. These runners will touch the surface with the ball of their foot but they immediately go back with their heel to the ground. This means that they do not build up optimal (although this is still better than heel striking) pre-tension in the arch of the foot, calf muscle, tendon and ligaments of the ankle. For me, this 'lazy' forefoot strike is also flat foot strike.

Mid-foot strike is actually flat foot strike

Midfoot strike is regularly mentioned when discussing running technique, but does it really exist? Personally, I believe not. There are two descriptions for midfoot strike.

1. The first is that midfoot strike is actually landing on the ball of the foot; however, as the ball of the foot is situated in the forefoot it can't be named midfoot strike.
2. Assuming that the midfoot is in between the heel and the ball of the foot, how can we land on that part without touching the ground with heel and ball of the foot at the same time? So, anyone practising this foot landing is actually a flat foot striker.

I can only conclude that there is no such thing as a midfoot landing.

Active forefoot strike

By my definition, a real forefoot striker is a runner who touches the surface first with the ball of the foot and, as their heel lowers towards the surface, they build up pre-tension in the arch of the foot, calf muscles, tendons and ligaments of the ankle. This is contrary to the 'lazy' forefoot striker who is actually more like a flat foot striker.

Most elite runners have this style of active forefoot striking, even during the marathon. With some runners it looks like they are striking with their heel first, but just before touching ground, at the very last moment, they pull their lower leg backwards which causes the forefoot striking the surface first.

An excellent example of forefoot striking can be seen with Kenyan runner Moses Mosop: youtube.com/watch?v=mTMgIViinuQ. This clip is from 30km into a marathon and clearly demonstrates a light, springy forefoot strike with his heel only 'kissing' the ground. Maybe forefoot *runner* is a better name for such an extremely active forefoot striker?

Lazy forefoot strike is probably the best choice for most runners

Running is not a quick kind of walking but more like springing from one foot to the other. Try jogging on the spot without shoes on and notice how your feet touch the ground. Now try to land on your heels first … it won't feel good. Therefore, landing on the ball of the foot seems the most natural style for very *fast* running. That is why for fast middle and long-distance runners (and for world class marathon runners) I would recommend an active forefoot strike.

A 'lazy' forefoot strike is probably best for the average and slower runner who races over 5km and longer. 'Lazy' forefoot striking should not be understood as a negative judgement, because for most runners this is the most economical and safest running style: it is less stressful for the Achilles tendon and calf muscles compared to the elite runner's style of active forefoot striking. Nevertheless, it could be worth trying to change to a more active forefoot strike as you may find you achieve a more reactive stride.

Note that a real heel striker experiences most of the impact forces in the knees, while an active forefoot striker will have the greatest forces in their feet, Achilles and calves. You will need quite some time to adapt to the latter and may experience soreness in your calves initially.

forefoot strike   *heel strike*

Changing your foot strike

Happily, the Easy Interval Method is perfect for helping you to change your foot strike. By regularly doing easy interval workouts over distances of 200 and 400m along with your strides, you will gradually develop more strength and reactivity in your feet, Achilles and calves. In this way you will naturally change your running style. For some runners this might mean a transition from a heel strike to *just* a 'lazy' forefoot strike, while others will be able to adapt to an active forefoot strike. Obviously, you need to transition very carefully. Start with forefoot landing during your warm-up for a few weeks. Next you might do a few repetitions during an easy 400m interval workout, preferably on a soft surface like grass. Gradually build this up and be patient. It might take many months to become a 'lazy' forefoot striker and consider not changing further if you are heavily built and/or a slower runner. A faster runner should try to change to an active forefoot strike. It might take a year or more to get used to performing an active forefoot strike during all your workouts without suffering stiff calf muscle the following days. If you experience sore calves, wait until this pain is gone before doing your next workout with your new forefoot strike.

Shoes without heel lift

In order to optimise the building up of elastic pre-tension, a runner should preferably race and train in shoes with as little heel lift as possible, preferably zero. Such shoes are often called 'minimalistic shoes'. A zero heel height means that the forefoot bed and heel of a shoe are the same height.

A runner in the Netherlands e-mailed me the following positive experience with running in shoes without any net heel lift: *"In recent years I have benefited greatly from the gradual transition to minimalistic shoes. This also helps me to run more smoothly. My experience is that running in light weight, flexible shoes with thin soles is very good for developing a flexible and reactive running style. Moreover, I finally got rid of years of Achilles tendon complaints."*

Two possible explanations for the latter: first the Achilles tendon and calf muscles are stressed more and therefore eventually get stronger. Secondly, wearing shoes with a thin sole and no net heel lift will cause less sideways movement (pronation); the thicker the sole, the greater the chance of sideways movements and hence injuries.

Coach Lex van Eck van der Sluijs calls shoes with a high net heel lift and a lot of cushioning 'pamper shoes'. My coach Herman Verheul had the same opinion: he was in favour of training in spikes (on the track and off road) without any heel lift. And let's not forget to mention the famous British runner Gordon Pirie, former 5000m world-record holder in the 1950s, who was also an advocate of forefoot striking and running in shoes with thin soles: "Running equals springing through the air, landing elastically on the forefoot with a flexed knee..."

Some more tips

Regularly do some exercises with a skipping rope or other bouncing exercises before or after your main session. Try to gradually change to training in racing flats or preferably minimalistic shoes. Again, do not go straight into it. Maybe try one session in flats/minimalist shoes and then the next one or two (until your legs feel okay) use your regular trainers.

One of my athletes (800-1500m) practiced heel striking for many years on advice given to him. Changing to an active forefoot landing took him two months and many days of stiff, even slightly painful calf muscles, but in the end he was enthusiastic about his new, smooth and more reactive running style. I have read many positive experiences: better running style and in the longer term, fewer injuries. Coach Lex van Eck van der Sluijs calls the process of changing: 'to be born again'.

Warning: in case you are a prominent heel striker and heavily built, it might be that you are not suited for active forefoot landing. Also when you are an older runner, changing your style might bring serious injury risks: so take more time for the process or don't do it.

Arms, shoulders, hands, rotation of torso

I have often heard how coaches shouted at their athletes to 'pull at their arms' during races. This is based on the idea that a faster arm movement would result in a faster pace of the legs. However, I advocate the idea (based on my experience) that arms should move in the rhythm of the legs and not vice versa. In particular, when you 'pull the arms in a final sprint', it will disturb your coordination: don't do it. Keep your shoulders low and your arms relaxed, with an angle of around 90 degrees between upper and lower arm. In many runners this angle may vary a little bit: a few degrees greater at the rearward compared to the forward swinging. Your hand is closed, but fingers remain relaxed, your thumb rests relaxed on your closed forefinger; don't make a fist.

When running there will be a minor rotation of your torso; it is impossible to hold it still. A more important aspect to focus on is trying to hold your torso straight up and firm or slightly forward, as opposed to hunching too far forward. Most elite runners lean slightly forward.

In chapter 5.3 I discussed a few exercises to improve reactivity and running economy. While it's clearly very important that you have strong, well-trained legs, every other muscle must also be exercised to achieve maximum performance. You should try to keep your entire body strong and balanced, which is why I advise all runners who train regularly to perform a basic whole-body strength routine 2-3 times a week. Added to this, I would also advocate serious runners to go to the gym once a week and use various machines (e.g. lower back machine - see figure 7 on page 151) to work on all-round body strength and conditioning.

Make your lower back strong and 'loose'

A weak core can result in reduced running economy and greater risk of injuries. A strong lower back is just as important as a strong stomach so make sure you are targeting all the muscles around your back and pelvis.

I came across a top regional runner who struggled with hamstring problems for many years but it was actually his weak core and pelvis that were causing his issues. Unfortunately it took 18 months before the correct diagnosis was made. After working on his core stability his hamstring problems were solved.

Crawling backwards up-hill. Photo: Klaas Lok

However, your lower back shouldn't just be strong; your vertebrae should also be 'loose'. If the movement between any of the vertebrae in your lower back (e.g. the S1–L5 joint) is limited, this could cause lower back pain and/or negatively influence your running. My coach Herman Verheul gave us many different kinds of exercises to achieve both a strong core as well as a 'loose' lower back. These exercises often combined both strength and movement simultaneously. This combination is important in order to train the small muscles around your vertebrae, which – according to medical experts – are very important for preventing lower back pain.

Verheul advocated some slightly unique exercises such as crawling on our hands and feet – both belly up and belly down – as well as what are now commonly called 'planks', in which we would lift opposite hands and legs off the ground (figure 4a, 4b) while trying to maintain a strong and stable core. A 'killer' exercise was crawling backwards up a very steep hill (much steeper than the photo suggests): it took me three years before I was able to complete the full 30m without resting in between. These exercises challenged our bodies in a totally different way to just normal running and provided us with more overall body strength.

Balancing
Although running is in a forward motion, it is important to strengthen your lateral (side) muscles as well, which will help create a more stable running motion. A good exercise is to balance on one foot and swing the other leg forward and backward. When you get really good, try and do it with your eyes closed! Another good balancing exercise: sideways jumping like ice-speed skaters do. Spring from one leg to the other in a lateral motion; during landing on your left foot, you try to touch the ground with your right hand – and vice versa. This is also a good exercise for your lower back.

Tiredness in arms
In very long distance races it is not uncommon for runners to complain of fatigue in their arms or shoulders. Stretching out your shoulders by gripping both hands behind your back, as well as performing all kind of crawling exercises (such as crab walk - figure 3a, 3b, 3c) will help improve your arm and shoulder fitness, and help avoid these issues.

Stretching
The effectiveness of stretching is still fiercely debated amongst both athletes and the scientific community. My personal experience is that mild, dynamic stretching for your calf muscles, upper leg muscles, lower back muscles and muscles around the pelvis is important to prevent injuries. It will also make your muscles relax and feel looser. Personally, I don't consider mild stretching as stretching, but just as making your muscles 'loose' and maintaining your natural range of movement. Don't forget you are a distance runner; you are not training to jump over hurdles. Don't do a lot of real stretching shortly before a race: you need a sound, normal tension in your muscles (overstretched muscles could temporarily be a bit weaker). I oppose static stretching: that is unnatural and not in accordance with the

normal functioning of your muscles. Because most people are already familiar with stretching and many examples of stretching exercises can be found on the internet, I refrain from giving examples in this book.

Coordination exercises

Many track & field clubs nowadays are very insistent on their runners performing drills and coordination exercises such as skipping, high knees, heel-to-bum kicks, etc. The point of these exercises is to try and increase the runner's reactivity and improve their stride, but that is the essence of the Easy Interval Method and so I feel by running easy intervals you will naturally develop a reactive stride and knee lift that will fit with your race speed. Furthermore, you will also be able to apply the proper technique when accelerating and sprinting. Only runners with real discrepancies in their gait should adjust their style with special coordination exercises.

Famous Finnish runner Lasse Viren, four-times Olympic champion (5000 & 10,000m in 1972 and 1976), ran with a so-called 'shuffle' - he barely lifted his knees at all. That all changed in the finishing laps when he unleashed his devastating sprint finish.

Examples of exercises-DVD

We had many different exercises, but they would take an entire book to describe. I have listed some in the next paragraph, but two of my former teammates are working on producing a DVD based on these exercises which they are hoping will be released by the end of 2019. I will inform you via my website: www.easyintervalmethod.com. The intro video can be watched here: https://www.youtube.com/watch?v=JchS1SGwW90&

Just a few exercises:
- To loosen your lower back: jog and every three or five steps bend over and - while still running - touch the ground with one hand, then straighten up, jog a few steps and then touch the ground with the other hand.
- Wheel-barrow walk (photo on page 76).
- Push-ups.
- Sit-ups.
- V-sits (figure 1).
- Crouching tiger (figure 2a, 2b).
- Crawling on hands and feet: sideward, backward or forward - belly up (crab walk - figure 3a, 3b, 3c) or belly down (bear crawl).
- Lift left hand and right foot; next right hand and left foot (figure 4a, 4b).
- Planking, belly down or side down (figure 5 and 6).
- To strengthen your lower back muscles (figure 7).
- Crawling on hands and feet, backward, belly down, uphill (see photo at page 147).
- Stand on one leg and swing the other forward and backward.
- Stand on one leg and circle the other leg.
- Circle your hips.

Figure 1
V-sits

Crouching tiger

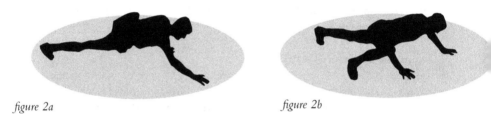

figure 2a   *figure 2b*

Crab walk, on hands and feet – belly up: sideward, backward or forward.

figure 3a   *figure 3b*

figure 3c

Lift left hand and right foot; next right hand and left foot

figure 4a

figure 4b

figure 5

Front plank

figure 6

Side plank

figure 7

Strengthening lower back muscles.
This exercise can also be done on a
chair with your feet under a table.

16. Triathlon, duathlon and easy interval training

Can the Easy Interval Method also be used for triathlon and duathlon? The answer is a resounding 'yes!' I have long thought that many of these athletes do not have very good running economy or reactivity. Short interval training is great for triathletes as their aerobic endurance is often very high from years of cycling. Some triathletes have switched to Easy Interval Method and reported substantial progress in their running. Here are three comments:

- A triathlete who focuses on running during winter time: "The Easy Interval Method works well for me. I am noticeably much fitter after a workout as well as after races and I rarely have any bad races anymore, even though my racing frequency is higher than ever. Last year has been the best year in my modest sports career, thanks to this way of training".

- "I did a lot of steady-state training, but at a certain point I didn't progress anymore. At that time I ran 3km in 10:34, but after five months training according to the Easy Interval Method I had improved to 9:50. Now in a sprint triathlon I can run 5km in 17:30 which is faster than I used to be able to do for a straight 5km run! I am very happy with all this progress."

- "I think this method is very interesting, especially for triathletes due to the fact that a triathlete is training for three sports and hence already doing so much aerobic endurance. After four months training easy intervals, I lowered my best time at 10km by a minute, although my total running mileage is less. I also noticed a positive effect on my frequent injuries".

World Cross-Country Championships in 1980. Klaas Lok, followed by French runners Alex Gonzales (456) and François Person (458), next Eddy de Pauw (Belgium) and Valeriy Sapon (Soviet Union).
Photo: Theo van de Rakt

17. Epilogue

Unfortunately, many runners find it hard to trust in this way of training; many don't have the courage to train in a lighter way, scared and insecure about not training hard enough. Athletes will often apply the logic that when you want to run fast in a race and want to stand the pain during racing, you have to train hard and suffer a lot. One key aspect I would point out is that, although each individual session in the Easy Interval Method is much lighter to a 'traditional' session, the overall cumulative quality is often much greater due to the frequency of faster running. As mentioned before, try adding up the total mileage of 'quality' (around marathon pace and faster) for a week's worth of training using your traditional schedule compared to a week using the Easy Interval Method. You will probably find that you accumulate far more 'quality' miles during the latter. However, don't make this mistake: performing three sessions a week of 6x1000m at just under lactate threshold pace is great quality, but doing three sessions of 6km fast endurance running per week (for many weeks) can be exhausting and wrong for many athletes.

Never trying out this method could be a real pity, because - considering the surprising progress of runners who changed to the Easy Interval Method - one can only conclude

FBK Games in the Netherlands, 1984. With one lap to go Wolf Dieter Poschmann (Germany) is leading ahead of Klaas Lok in the 5000m. In third position Steve Plasencia (USA). Lok wins in 13:41. Photo: Conno du Fossé

that many runners who train 'traditional' might *never* reach their maximal potential.

My advice is to at least give it a try. If you are a track runner then perhaps try it at the end of a race season and see how you feel. And to coaches, I quote the words of coach Lex van Eck van der Sluijs: "If you don't run yourself anymore, just let your runners train according to this method and at a certain moment they will tell you why it works".

I hope it is clear that the core of the programme is important. It is essential that the basic training is easy interval training instead of steady-state training. The actual distances used are generally a guide and should not be hard and fast rules. Whether you use 200, 400, 1000m or 150, 300m and a mile or even timed intervals are of minor importance. It's the principle that is the most important thing I am trying to emphasise - steady-state training may not be the most effective way to train for endurance running. You can decide how much extra you add to this basic programme: more interval training (e.g. 8-10 or maybe even 12x1000m occasionally), some more endurance training and/or anaerobic training, depending on your favourite distance, your 'training age' and so on.

I repeat the warning written several times in this book: control yourself regarding the speed of the basic easy interval training. When you frequently run your intervals a little too fast, you may get overtrained. This may go mostly unnoticed in training, but your race results will be negatively affected and you run the risk of injury.

I do hope that after reading this book you will be familiar with the insights into the how and why of the Easy Interval Method. I also sincerely hope that this book will make a positive contribution to both your running performance as well as your running pleasure, and I wish you all the best.

Klaas Lok